"Kyndra's new cookbook is absolutely essential for anyone searching for an amazingly flavorful path to health. Her recipes are not just delicious; they are made with ingredients that are familiar and nutritious!"

—MARIA EMMERICH, author of *Keto Adapted* and creator of Maria Mind Body Health

"Kyndra has hit all the right notes! Her mouthwatering recipes and beautiful photography will make you wish you could reach into the page and take a bite. I especially love the refreshing honesty regarding her low-carb journey, which so many of us can relate to."

—MELLISSA SEVIGNY, creator of the blog I Breathe, I'm Hungry

"This book is all about making comfort food accessible again. Pizza, waffles, biscuits and gravy, yes it is all here. This will quickly become one of the most dog-eared, food-spattered cookbooks in your collection."

—CAROLYN KETCHUM, creator of the blog All Day I Dream About Food

"This book will have your mouth watering and your palate satisfied with healthy meals your whole family will love. Not only are the recipes easy to make, you can find most ingredients at your local grocery store. This book is a must have for every low-carb kitchen!"

—VANESSA ROMERO creator of the blog Healthy Living How To

"*The Primal Low-Carb Kitchen* is a fantastic resource for low-carb enthusiasts. With it's wonderful resource section, it will teach you how to do low-carb the healthy way! Learn how to swap out your old favorite ingredients for healthy alternatives, how to identify hidden sources of gluten and how to save money on your groceries.

—ARSY VARTANIAN, author of *The Paleo Foodie Cookbook* and *The Paleo Slow Cooker*

"Kyndra Holley is like a comfort food wizard. She takes the most beloved meals from your childhood, and turns them into healthier masterpieces right before your eyes."

—CINDY SEXTON, author of *Paleo Takes 5 -or- Fewer* and creator of PALEOdISH.com

"Enjoy comfort foods at their low-carb finest, while incorporating the nutrient-dense values Paleo offers. Discover the healthiest *you* without leaving behind the foods you love thanks to *The Primal Low-Carb Kitchen!*"

—CIARRA HANNAH, author of *The Frugal Paleo Cookbook* and creator of the blog Popular Paleo

"Imagine yourself eating a low-carb, Primal version of mac and cheese. How about a waffle breakfast sandwich? Kyndra has those recipes for you and so much more! If you're looking for a healthier version of your favorite comfort foods, this cookbook is a must have in your kitchen!"

—JENNY CASTANEDA, creator of Paleo Foodie Kitchen and author of *One-Pot Paleo*

TO ALL OF THE BACON LOVERS WHO HAVE FOLLOWED MY BLOG AND SHOWN THEIR SUPPORT OVER THE YEARS. WITHOUT ALL OF YOU, NONE OF THIS WOULD BE POSSIBLE.

PAGE STREET
PUBLISHING CO.

Copyright © 2015 Kyndra Holley

First published in 2015 by
Page Street Publishing Co.
27 Congress Street, Suite 103
Salem, MA 01970
www.pagestreetpublishing.com

Distributed by Macmillan; sales in Canada by The Canadian Manda Group; distribution in Canada by The Jaguar Book Group.

17   16   15   18   1   2   3   4   5

ISBN-13: 978-1-62414-119-5
ISBN-10: 1-62414-119-6

Library of Congress Control Number: 2014956899

Cover and book design by Page Street Publishing Co.
Photography by Kyndra Holley

Printed and bound in China

Page Street is proud to be a member of 1% for the Planet. Members donate one percent of their sales to one or more of the over 1,500 environmental and sustainability charities across the globe who participate in this program.

THE PRIMAL LOW-CARB KITCHEN

COMFORT FOOD RECIPES FOR THE CARB CONSCIOUS COOK

KYNDRA HOLLEY

FOUNDER OF PEACE, LOVE AND LOW CARB

PAGE STREET
PUBLISHING CO.

CONTENTS

SOUPS AND SALADS 95

SIDES AND SNACKS 123

BREAKFAST 153

DRESSINGS AND SAUCES 173

FOREWORD

Kyndra Holley and I have been orbiting around each other in the low-carb universe for years. As I was doing research for my blog, looking for people sharing quality information about low-carb nutrition, I found Peace, Love and Low Carb and immediately connected with Kyndra Holley's amazing story of triumph over weight and health that reminded me of my own successful transformation journey. I immediately connected with her approach—a "clean" low-carb diet that doesn't include processed foods and doesn't sacrifice taste.

After losing 180 pounds on the Atkins diet in 2004, I eventually came to realize that the processed foods—Atkins bars, low-carb pastas, low-carb breads and more—were clearly not healthy over the long term, and although they were low-carb, I was still feeding into my carb addiction. That's when I adopted the same philosophy Kyndra shares in this book. Choosing the highest quality grass-fed meats, organic vegetables, high-fat dairy, nuts and seeds, and superior dietary fats like grass-fed butter, coconut oil and lard were the keys to elevating my game even more on my own low-carb diet. I've been sharing this philosophy with my own readers ever since.

With the meteoric rise in popularity of ancestral-based Paleo and Primal diets over the past few years, many of us longtime low-carb enthusiasts have gone beyond simply looking at limiting carbohydrates and now desire to improve the quality of the food we are consuming. This means our healthy low-carb lifestyle is comprised of real, whole, nourishing foods that would be recognized by our great-grandmas as "food." It's a logical next step for anyone who has consumed a low-carb diet to gradually begin to clean up the foods they are consuming to the best quality possible they can afford. Understandably, it can be a hard road for many because of budget constraints, societal pressure about food and the familiarity with purchasing foods that are convenient and easy.

What Kyndra has done in *The Primal Low-Carb Kitchen* is empower people eating a low-carb diet to make the lateral shift over to eating a Paleo or Primal nutritional template with a low-carb emphasis. Her focus is on real, whole, unprocessed foods, and thanks to her foodie background, low-carb readers making the transition to a more Primal way of eating will see tremendous positive changes in their health without missing any of their favorite comfort foods.

Because Kyndra's been there herself, she demonstrates how simple the low-carb to Primal-low-carb shift can be. It helps that she has an eye for making comforting recipes that will have your mouth watering and yet be so very good for you too.

You know it's time to clean up your low-carb diet, or perhaps begin it in earnest on the right foot. When you're ready to give it a shot, this is your go-to manual for making it happen. Lay aside all the excuses for not doing it, and let Kyndra pass along the "been there, done that" wisdom she has amassed. Relax, enjoy the process, be kind to yourself and never forget you and your health are worth the effort. YOU CAN DO IT!

—Jimmy Moore
author of *Keto Clarity* and *Cholesterol Clarity* and host of "The Livin' La Vida Low-Carb Show"

Jimmy Moore

INTRODUCTION

Peace, love and low carb—Three simple words that brought profound changes in my life. It was hard to be at peace and to love myself when I was so overweight and unhealthy that I could barely stand to look at the person staring back at me in the mirror. This wasn't my first rodeo when it came to diet and exercise. In the past, I lost 50 pounds (23 kg) through a low-carb way of eating. I maintained for about a year and then gained it all back, plus some. I didn't go about it in a very healthy way. I wasn't eating nutrient-dense, whole foods, and I hadn't completely cut out grains and gluten. I was only concerned with the carbohydrate count and not with the overall nutritional content of the food I was eating. I was still eating a lot of highly processed, packaged foods, full of ingredients that I couldn't even begin to pronounce. I pretty much survived off bacon cheeseburgers without the bun and salads topped with so much ranch dressing that there was no lettuce to be seen. I was one of those people that helped give low-carb diets a bad rap. Despite my poor nutrition, the weight came off fairly effortlessly, and I wasn't even working out. This experience gave me a false sense of what living a healthy lifestyle actually looked like. I equated health with weight and felt I was being healthy simply because I was losing weight. Throughout all the years I spent being unhappy and overweight, I tried every fad diet out there. I was always looking for a quick fix. I was enamored by celebrity fad diets, infomercials, magic pills, lotions, potions and promises of a 24-hour fix. I was willing to try everything except eating healthy and working out.

Then one day, almost out of nowhere, I woke up. I started to see food differently. I realized what I had already known all along. I didn't put on all this weight overnight, and I certainly wasn't going to lose it all overnight, either. If I wanted results, I was going to have to put in the work. I knew it would take sheer determination and an abundance of willpower to make it happen. I finally felt ready to commit to change. My views on food had begun to shift, and I became increasingly aware of what I was putting in my body. The days of bunless burgers and only counting carbs were behind me. That is not to say that I don't still love a good bunless burger with ranch dressing; I just eat other things in addition to that now, and when I want a dressing, I make it from scratch so that I know exactly what is in it.

I love food. I always have. I love eating food. I love photographing food. I even love just being around food. Food is one of the only things that can truly delight all of the senses at once. What's not to love? I'd been working in restaurants for more years than I like to account for, and that meant that I was constantly surrounded by my drug of choice. Even though I never worked in the kitchen at any of those restaurants, I spent a lot of time there because I loved watching the whole process unfold. As a manager I got to see every step of the action. I got to check-in the delivery of fresh foods, watch them being prepped in the back kitchen, see them hit the line for the chefs to work their magic on, stand side by side with the food expeditor to be the final approval of quality, whisk the food away to the guests, watch them eat it and check back only to be met with oohs and aahs of how incredible their meal was. It is quite a visceral process.

By working in a handful of fine dining establishments, I was exposed to ingredients and cooking techniques that I never knew existed. I grew up in a very "meat and potatoes, salt and pepper" home. All meat was cooked well-done, and ketchup was our only condiment. Working in restaurants, not only was I exposed to a variety of new ingredients, but I was also tasting many of them for the first time. More often than not, it was love at first bite. My palate grew to be more sophisticated over time. I was able to go out for a nice meal, analyze the flavor profiles and quickly identify a majority of the ingredients. I began cooking at home a lot more, and I mean *really* cooking, not just heating things up. Each time I created a new dish, it fueled my passion until I felt fully ignited. Food was no longer a torture mechanism. It was no longer an anchor weighing me down, literally and figuratively. I found my catapult to change.

I was determined to change my life without sacrificing all the foods I so dearly loved, and so began my mission to re-create all of my favorite comfort foods into primal low-carb versions! I started with mac and cheese, the same "mac" and cheese recipe that you will find in this book. From there I moved on to pizza, chips, potatoes, biscuits and so forth . . . and it just spread like wildfire from there. I started taking pictures of my cooking adventures and thus my blog was born.

As my food priorities changed, so did my waistline. The weight started coming off again. I was finding out that it was in fact possible to love food and to love myself at the same time. I was no longer just counting carbs with a complete disregard for everything else on the label. I finally ditched grains and went gluten-free. I had made the shift to a primal low-carb way of life and big things were starting to happen. I knew then that I was on to something. Something that could change the course of my life forever.

Every time I step into the kitchen, it is as if I have a fresh canvas waiting to be painted. I can't explain how it feels to dream up a new recipe, bring it to life and then get to share it with others all around the world. Watching someone eat something I created is a moment of pure joy for me. Every day I learn something new about food and something new about myself. I feel truly blessed to be able to share all of that with you.

Peace and Love,

Kyndra D Holley

RESOURCES

The theme of this book is *comfort.* That extends beyond just the recipes.
I want you to feel comfortable being in the kitchen and comfortable in your
primal low-carb lifestyle. This opening chapter is full of great resources to help
you do just that. From uncovering hidden sources of gluten to simple swaps,
this chapter has you covered.

HIDDEN SOURCES OF GLUTEN

Hidden gluten is all around us. It is lurking in some of the least likely of places. If you suffer from gluten insensitivity or intolerance, it can be vitally important to be aware of potential sources of gluten that you may come in contact with on a daily basis. Did you know that a surprising amount of gluten is hidden in non-food-related items as well? Here is an outline of some of those sources.

- Artificial colors, such as caramel coloring
- Baby formula
- Baby powder
- Bacon, jerky, sausage, hot dogs and lunch meats
- Baking powder
- Beer
- Bouillon cubes, broths, seasonings and spices
- Canned beans
- Canned meats (tuna, chicken, beef, etc.)
- Canned soups
- Cheese spreads
- Chewing gum
- Colorings and flavorings
- Drywall
- Diet or weight-loss shakes
- Envelopes and stamps
- Food starch and modified food starch

- Frozen vegetables
- Glue
- Hard alcohol
- Hot chocolate
- Ice cream
- Imitation seafood
- Instant coffee
- Ketchup
- Licorice
- Lipstick
- Liquid smoke and smoke flavorings
- Lotions
- Malt
- Marinades
- Makeup
- Medications
- Mustard
- Non-dairy creamer
- Pickles and relish
- Potato chips

- Pre-made cocktail mixes
- Prescription drugs
- Protein powders
- Pudding
- Salad dressings, condiments, gravies and sauces
- Salami and other deli meats
- Shampoo
- Soy sauce
- Store-bought pasta sauces
- Store-bought spice mixes
- Sunblock
- Supplements
- Syrups
- Toothpaste
- Vinegars
- Vitamins
- Worcestershire sauce
- Yogurt

Here are several small steps you can take to make sure that you are not unknowingly gluten-dosing yourself:

- You can avoid accidental cross-contamination with gluten by thoroughly reading and inspecting nutrition labels and then researching ingredients you may not be familiar with.

- When dining out, do not hesitate to ask the server, chef or managers whether there is gluten in any of the dishes you are interested in. As someone who worked in the restaurant industry for fifteen years, I highly recommend asking to speak to the chef directly. The chef will be the most knowledgeable person when it comes to the menu and its ingredients.

- When you are unsure, the easiest thing to do is just SKIP IT!

SIMPLE SWAPS

Switching to a primal low-carb lifestyle doesn't have to mean giving up your favorite foods. It simply means that sometimes it becomes necessary to get creative and think outside the box when it comes to healthy alternatives. I have compiled a list of creative solutions to leave you feeling satisfied, instead of deprived.

Bread—Gluten-free wraps and tortillas, lettuce wraps, portobello mushrooms

Breading—Parmesan cheese, pork rinds, almond flour, coconut flour, ground flaxseeds and chia seeds

Chips and crackers—Pork rinds, vegetable chips, cucumber slices, prosciutto crisps, pepperoni chips, cheese crisps, kale chips, Brussels sprout chips, sweet potato chips, dried seaweed snacks, nuts, jicama, fried green beans, sliced bell pepper

Croutons—Nuts, cheese crisps, fried gluten-free salami

Flour—Almond flour, coconut flour, flaxseed meal, protein powder, hazelnut flour, macadamia nut flour

French fries—Turnip, parsnip, rutabaga, sweet potato, zucchini

Hash browns—Grated zucchini, celeriac, rutabaga, grated cauliflower, carrot, sweet potato

Lasagna noodles—Sliced eggplant, sliced zucchini

Mashed potatoes—Cauliflower mash, celery root mash, whipped sweet potatoes

Milk—Almond milk, coconut milk, heavy cream

Pasta—Vegetable noodles, shredded cabbage, cauliflower florets, spaghetti squash, zucchini, shirataki noodles, kelp noodles

Pizza—Cauliflower pizza crust, pizza stuffed peppers, pizza chicken, pizza stuffed mushrooms, pizza casseroles

Rice—Grated zucchini, riced cauliflower, shirataki rice

Soy sauce—Gluten-free soy sauce, coconut aminos, tamari, liquid aminos

CREATIVE WAYS TO MAXIMIZE YOUR GROCERY BUDGET

- Ask stores whether they price match—this saves you from going to multiple stores.

- Avoid products placed at the end of store aisles and on checkout stands.

- Browse ad circulars each week and shop according to the sales.

- Buy discounted meats and freeze them.

- Buy generic equivalents instead of shopping by brand name.

- Buy groceries with cash or debit cards and skip the high-interest credit cards.

- Buy in bulk whenever possible.

- Buy your meat from a butcher or buy an entire animal at a time.

- Grow your own garden.

- Join a CSA or local co-op for your produce.

- Make freezer meals in large quantities.

- Make your meals from scratch instead of buying packaged meals—skip the convenience cost and the additives.

- Meal plan before shopping.

- Repurpose leftovers into new meals.

- Search top and bottoms shelves for less expensive items—the most expensive products are usually in the middle at eye level.

- Shop farmers' markets.

- Shop for produce according to season and don't be afraid to buy frozen.

- Shop multiple stores when necessary to maximize the savings.

- Shop the perimeter of the store—fresh produce, meats and dairy are on the perimeter, whereas junk food normally lines the shelves of the inner aisles.

- Stick to your list.

- Stock up on sale items for products you use regularly.

- Subscribe to store reward programs.

- Take advantage of your vacuum sealer.

- Use coupons.

HOW TO INCREASE YOUR GROCERY BUDGET WITHOUT INCREASING YOUR TOTAL MONTHLY EXPENSES

- Cancel memberships you aren't actually using regularly—gym, wine clubs, media streaming, magazine subscriptions, etc.

- Cancel your cable services.

- Carpool, ride the bus, walk or bike to work.

- Consign unwanted or unused household items.

- Consolidate or refinance loans wherever possible.

- DIY whenever possible.

- Do regularly scheduled maintenance on your vehicles to avoid costly repairs.

- Host an evening of friends and fun instead of going out.

- Keep your home 1 degree cooler when you are home and turn off the thermostat when you leave.

- Negotiate interest rates with credit card companies.

- Only do full loads of laundry and dishes, to save on electricity.

- Outfit your home with energy-efficient lightbulbs.

- Pack a lunch for work instead of going out to eat.

- Reassess wants versus needs.

- Restructure cell phone plans and comparison-shop different providers.

- Skip the daily stop at your local coffee stand.

- Split entrées and skip drinks and desserts when dining out.

- Trade services with others, based on skills and talents.

- Watch movies at home and enjoy your own snacks.

- When dining out, take advantage of happy hours and restaurant promotions.

MY KITCHEN MUST-HAVES

Box grater—Four-sided box graters are an inexpensive but valuable tool to have in your kitchen. Each side is different, allowing you to zest, grate, shred and even slice.

Cast-iron pans—Cast-iron pans are such a solid investment because they will easily outlive all of us. My mom still has the same cast-iron pans from when I was born. Not a lot of things in this world are affordable and can stand the test of time. They are naturally nonstick, can grill and sauté and even withstand the heat of an oven.

Colanders—Colanders are another inexpensive kitchen necessity. Not only are they useful for draining such things as vegetable noodles and cauliflower rice, but they are also great for washing fresh produce and steaming vegetables and can even prolong the life of moisture-sensitive vegetables, such as mushrooms, when used for fridge storage.

Food processor—What don't food processors do? My most common uses are making low-carb breading mixtures, making cauliflower rice, grinding nuts and making nut butters, pureeing soups and mixing dressings and sauces. It even has a grating feature, which is incredibly handy for grating vegetables or large amounts of cheese.

Food scale—A good food scale will prevent a great number of kitchen disasters. It will help keep your recipes accurate, make conversions a breeze and help you practice portion control.

Garbage bowl—You can use any old large bowl for this. It is so handy to keep a bowl in the center of all the action to put all your unwanted wrappers and scraps into. It saves you from making multiple trips to the garbage can while preparing your meals.

Lots and lots of cutting boards—I am a cutting board junkie. I have a variety of wooden ones, along with glass, plastic and marble. When I set out for a day of cooking, I usually cover my counter with cutting boards. Using a separate cutting board for different food groupings helps cut down on the potential of cross-contamination of foods. You would hate to serve someone fresh vegetables that had come into contact with raw chicken.

Nested stainless steel mixing bowls with lids—Having a variety of different-size mixing bowls really comes in handy when you are making more than one dish at a time. Stainless-steel bowls are easy to clean and last a long time. They will be hanging out with your cast-iron pans, long after you are gone. Getting a set that includes lids comes in handy for making a dish and transporting it in the same bowl.

Parchment paper—Parchment makes clean up a cinch for anything you bake, including those full sheet pans of bacon.

Pots and pans—A reliable set of cookware is a must. I suggest putting some research into this and saving up for a high-quality set. I personally have a Calphalon set, and I couldn't be happier with it.

Ramekins and pinch bowls—I use ramekins and pinch bowls daily. They are great for portioning out chopped veggies, shredded cheeses, seasonings and so on. It is a great way to prep and stage all the necessary ingredients for a recipe. The sets I have are also oven safe and come with lids. This makes them great for baking single portion items and also for storing leftover ingredients.

Rimmed baking sheets—Rimmed baking sheets are great all-purpose baking sheets. The rimmed sides prevent spillage. They are excellent for baking, roasting vegetables, cooking meats, you name it!

Rubber spatulas, wooden spoons and tongs—I often joke that if I were to lose a hand, I could easily get by with one of these as a substitution, especially the tongs. These are an indispensable part of my kitchen.

Slow cooker—Slow cookers are perfect for lazy fall and winter days. They do all the work for you. Toss the ingredients in, turn it on and let it go to work. They are also a great way to tenderize tougher cuts of meat. Cooking meat slowly and at a lower temperature makes even the toughest cuts fall to pieces.

Spiral slicer—A spiral slicer is a low-carber's best friend. The low-carb world changed forever with the introduction of vegetable noodles—so easy to make and such a great way to get more vegetables in your diet.

SIMPLE SEASONING BLENDS

It is really simple and even kind of fun to make your own spice blends. One of the many reasons I started doing this was because, as we covered earlier, many of the store-bought seasonings are not gluten-free. Not only do many of them contain gluten, but they also have a lot of nasty chemicals and additives to keep them from clumping and to extend their shelf life. Making your own seasoning blends is far more affordable and far better for your health. These are the staples that I always have on hand in my spice pantry. I whip up a batch as needed and just store them in an airtight container. I also like to double or triple the batches and give them out in mason jars as gifts!

TACO SEASONING

SERVING SIZE: 1 TSP

2 tbsp (20 g) chili powder

2 tbsp (15 g) ground cumin

2 tsp (5 g) onion powder

2 tsp (7 g) garlic powder

2 tsp (5 g) celery salt

½ tsp cayenne pepper

½ tsp black pepper

½ tsp garlic salt

PER SERVING: 9 Calories; trace Fat; trace Protein; 2g Carbohydrate; trace Dietary Fiber; 2g Net Carb

BLACKENED SEASONING

SERVING SIZE: 1 TSP

1½ tbsp (10 g) paprika

1 tbsp (10 g) garlic powder

1 tbsp (7 g) onion powder

1 tbsp (5 g) dried thyme

1 tsp cayenne pepper

1 tsp dried basil

1 tsp ground cumin

1 tsp celery salt

½ tsp dried oregano

PER SERVING: 6 Calories; trace Fat; trace Protein; 1g Carbohydrate; trace Dietary Fiber; 1g Net Carb

POULTRY SEASONING

SERVING SIZE: 1 TSP

1 tbsp (5 g) dried thyme

1 tbsp (2 g) rubbed sage

1 tbsp (10 g) dried onion flakes

1½ tsp (8 g) sea salt

1½ tsp (5 g) garlic powder

¾ tsp black pepper

PER SERVING: 4 Calories; trace Fat; trace Protein; 1g Carbohydrate; trace Dietary Fiber; 1g Net Carb

DRY ONION SOUP MIX

SERVING SIZE: 1 TSP

4 tbsp (40 g) dried onion flakes

2 tbsp (30 g) organic, gluten-free, powdered beef bouillon

1 tsp onion powder

1 tsp garlic powder

1 tsp dried parsley

¼ tsp celery salt

¼ tsp black pepper

PER SERVING: 10 Calories; trace Fat; trace Protein; 2g Carbohydrate; trace Dietary Fiber; 2g Net Carb

SEASONING SALT

SERVING SIZE: 1 TSP

3 tbsp (55 g) sea salt

1½ tsp (4 g) onion powder

1 tsp garlic powder

½ tsp paprika

½ tsp black pepper

PER SERVING: 2 Calories; trace Fat; trace Protein; trace Carbohydrate; trace Dietary Fiber; trace Net Carb

STEAK SEASONING

SERVING SIZE: 1 TSP

2 tbsp (40 g) sea salt

1 tbsp (10 g) + 1 tsp dried onion flakes

1½ tsp (4 g) paprika

1½ tsp (4 g) cracked black pepper

1 tsp granulated garlic

1 tsp granulated onion

1 tsp crushed red pepper flakes

½ tsp dried thyme

½ tsp celery salt

½ tsp dried cumin

PER SERVING: 3 Calories; trace Fat; trace Protein; 1g Carbohydrate; trace Dietary Fiber; 1g Net Carb

STARTERS

The starters or appetizers section is easily my favorite part of any menu or cookbook. Why? Because I love food! The portions are typically small and therefore, I can order multiple dishes without feeling guilty, or without crazy looks from service staff as I ramble off my vast list of selections.

My husband and I dine the same way. We just want to taste *everything*. We are a restaurant owner's dream come true. "The perfect check," as they call it in the industry: drinks, starters, salads, entrées, dessert, coffee. We hit all the courses. Before we know it, our bill looks as if a family of eight was just at our table. Recently we have changed our game plan a bit in an attempt to scale it down budget-wise and waistline-wise. Now we typically each get a salad and then share anywhere between two and four appetizers. That way we get to taste a little of everything without being tied down to one large main dish. The alternative would be going around to other tables and asking for bites of their dishes. No one wants that!

The other thing I love about starters is that it is the one course that brings everyone together. This is where the magic happens. It is the course made for sharing. Sharing of food and sharing of conversation. How many meaningful conversations have you had while sharing a plate of delicious food? Countless, right? One could argue that starters bring people together, even if only through a shared love of food.

This chapter has some new spins on classic favorites. Make some Loaded Sweet Potato Bites (page 19) and Baked Heirloom Caprese Salad with Bacon Vinaigrette (page 26), pour some wine and let the conversation flow.

LOADED SWEET POTATO BITES

One of my all-time favorite appetizers is and always has been potato skins. These sweet potato bites have all of the pizzazz of a potato skin but with a much lower carb count and pack a lot of essential vitamins and antioxidants into your diet. This is one of my favorite dishes to take to potluck-style parties. It is so simple but always manages to impress.

SERVES: 6

1 lb (455 g) sweet potato, sliced in ¼ inch (6 mm)-thick slices

3 tbsp (45 ml) olive oil, plus more if needed

Sea salt and black pepper, to taste

½ cup (60 g) sharp cheddar cheese, shredded

⅓ cup (40 g) sour cream

6 slices bacon, cooked crisp and crumbled

2 green onions, chopped

Preheat the oven to 400°F (205°C).

In a large mixing bowl, combine the sweet potato slices, olive oil, sea salt and black pepper. Toss until the sweet potatoes are well coated.

Line the sweet potato slices in a single layer on a rimmed baking sheet and bake on the top rack for 25 minutes.

Top each sweet potato with cheese, sour cream, bacon and green onion.

PER SERVING: 210 Calories; 15g Fat; 6g Protein; 14g Carbohydrate; 2g Dietary Fiber; 12g Net Carbs

ROASTED RED PEPPER AND SUN-DRIED TOMATO HUMMUS

The texture of a recipe can make or break it. The texture of this hummus is spot on. You could serve it to anyone and they wouldn't know they were eating zucchini in place of garbanzo beans. This is a family friendly dip that even your children will love.

SERVES: 10

2 medium zucchini, peeled and cubed

4 oz (115 g) roasted red peppers

¼ cup (15 g) sun-dried tomatoes

Juice of ½ lemon

¼ cup (60 g) creamy roasted tahini

3 large cloves garlic, minced

1 tbsp (15 ml) olive oil

1 tsp ground cumin

1 tsp sea salt, or more to taste

In a food processor, combine the zucchini, roasted red peppers, sun-dried tomatoes, lemon juice, tahini, garlic, olive oil, cumin and sea salt. Pulse until smooth and creamy.

Refrigerate for at least 1 hour prior to serving.

PER SERVING: 63 Calories; 5g Fat; 2g Protein; 5g Carbohydrate; 2g Dietary Fiber; Net Carbs 3g

BACON GUACAMOLE

This guacamole supports my belief that everything is better with bacon. The uses for this recipe are endless. I love to put it on my eggs, on top of burgers, dip fresh vegetables into it, and I especially love to eat it with fresh made cheese crisps. This tastes best if you cover it and refrigerate for an hour or more before serving.

SERVES: 18

4 large avocados, peeled, pitted and cubed

3 cloves garlic, minced

Juice of ½ small lime

2 tbsp (20 g) pickled jalapeño slices, chopped

¼ cup (65 g) medium-hot salsa

1½ tsp (4 g) minced onion flakes

½ tsp sea salt

Pinch of cayenne pepper

6 slices bacon, cooked crisp and crumbled

In a large mixing bowl, fork mash the avocados. Add the garlic, lime juice, jalapeño, salsa, onion flakes, sea salt and cayenne pepper. Continue mashing and mixing until all the ingredients are well incorporated. Stir in the bacon crumbles.

PER SERVING: 87 Calories; 8g Fat; 2g Protein; 4g Carbohydrate; 1g Dietary Fiber; 3g Net Carbs

OLIVE SALAD

One of my favorite cities in the world is New Orleans. I have been there more times than anywhere outside of my own city. One of the staples of the city is Muffuletta (page 64). It is a jumbo-size sandwich made on fresh Sicilian bread with sesame seeds. The sandwich is filled with Italian meats and cheeses and a hearty portion of terrifically briny olive salad. This recipe is my take on that olive salad. I love to add it to scrambled eggs, mix it into my salads and make meat roll-ups with it.

SERVES: 20

1½ cups (250 g) giardiniera pickled vegetables

1 cup (135 g) green olives

1 cup (135 g) Kalamata olives

½ cup (45 g) pepperoncini

⅓ cup (80 ml) red wine vinegar

¼ cup (35 g) roasted red peppers

¼ cup (60 ml) olive oil

4 large cloves garlic

1 tsp dried oregano

1 tsp dried basil

½ tsp black pepper

½ cup (70 g) capers

In a food processor, combine the giardiniera, green olives, Kalamata olives, pepperoncini, red wine vinegar, roasted red peppers, olive oil and garlic. Pulse until all the ingredients are roughly chopped. Stir in the oregano, basil, black pepper and capers. Mix until well incorporated.

Stir in the capers. Cover and refrigerate for at least 1 hour before serving.

PER SERVING: 56 Calories; 5g Fat; trace Protein; 2g Carbohydrate; trace Dietary Fiber; 2g Net Carbs

TIP: This salad tastes better the longer it has time to sit and let the flavors come together. You can store it in the fridge in an airtight container for up to 3 weeks.

BAKED HEIRLOOM CAPRESE SALAD WITH BACON VINAIGRETTE

Caprese is typically served as a cold dish, but I thought I'd change things up a bit and create a warm and inviting, baked version. I serve it family style, right off the baking sheet. The bacon fat vinaigrette absolutely makes this dish. I bet you will think twice about discarding the fat drippings next time you cook bacon.

SERVES: 6

6 slices bacon, cooked crisp and crumbled, 3 tbsp (35 g) fat drippings reserved

3 tbsp (45 ml) balsamic vinegar

2 tbsp (30 ml) olive oil

2 lbs (910 g) heirloom tomatoes, cut into ½ inch (1.3 cm)-thick slices

3 cloves garlic, thinly sliced

12 oz (340 g) fresh mozzarella, cut into ½ inch (1.3 cm)-thick slices

15 fresh basil leaves

Sea salt and black pepper, to taste

Preheat the oven to 300°F (177°C). Line a rimmed baking sheet with parchment paper.

In a small mixing bowl, combine the bacon fat, balsamic vinegar and olive oil. Whisk together with a fork.

Line the tomato slices in a single layer across the parchment paper and top with the sliced garlic.

Top the tomatoes with fresh mozzarella slices, bacon crumbles and fresh basil leaves.

Drizzle the bacon vinaigrette mixture over the top of the entire sheet and sprinkle with sea salt and black pepper.

Bake for 30 minutes.

PER SERVING: 343 Calories; 28g Fat; 15g Protein; 9g Carbohydrate; 2g Dietary Fiber; 7g Net Carbs

ALMOND PARMESAN ZUCCHINI FRIES

Preparing zucchini this way really brings out a sweetness that you can't seem to find in other zucchini recipes. Not only will these zucchini fries make you feel as if you are no longer missing out on French fries, but it is a terrific way to sneak in more vegetables.

SERVES: 6

4 medium zucchini (about 2 lbs [910 g])

1½ tsp (8 g) sea salt

2 large eggs

¾ cup (75 g) almond flour

½ cup (50 g) Parmesan cheese, grated

1 tbsp (5 g) Italian seasoning

1½ tsp (4 g) onion powder

1½ tsp (5 g) garlic powder

Preheat the oven to 425°F (219°C). Line a rimmed baking sheet with parchment paper.

Cut the zucchini into fry-size sticks. Lay the zucchini sticks in a single layer on top of paper towels. Sprinkle the zucchini with 1 teaspoon of sea salt. Top with another layer of paper towels. The salt will help draw out excess moisture from the zucchini, which will help the breading stay on. Let stand for about 15 minutes and then dab the zucchini dry with a paper towel.

Crack the eggs into a shallow bowl and fork whisk.

In a separate, large shallow bowl, combine the almond flour, Parmesan cheese, Italian seasoning, onion powder, garlic powder and remaining ½ teaspoon sea salt. Mix until all the ingredients are well incorporated.

Dip the zucchini sticks in the egg wash and then dredge them in the breading mixture. Make sure that each stick is well coated and line them in a single layer on the prepared baking sheet.

Bake for 15 minutes, flip and then bake for an additional 15 minutes.

PER SERVING: 161 Calories; 11g Fat; 10g Protein; 9g Carbohydrate; 3g Dietary Fiber; 6g Net Carbs

GARLIC-PARMESAN BRUSSELS SPROUT CHIPS

I love finding healthy low-carb alternatives to chips that the whole family will eat. These delicate leaves pack a big crunch. This just might be the dish that converts those non-sprout-eating members of your family. They also make for a vitamin-packed, portable snack.

SERVES: 6

2 lbs (910 g) Brussels sprouts

¼ cup (60 ml) olive oil

¼ cup (25 g) Parmesan cheese, grated

1½ tsp (5 g) garlic powder

1 tsp sea salt

½ tsp black pepper

Preheat the oven to 350°F (177°C). Line a rimmed baking sheet with parchment paper.

Trim the bottoms of the Brussels sprouts and discard any brown, wilted leaves. Peel the outermost leaves from the Brussels sprouts to use for your chips. Discard the core of the sprout, or chop up and save for later use.

In a large mixing bowl, toss the sprout leaves with olive oil, Parmesan cheese, garlic powder, sea salt and black pepper.

Line the coated leaves in a single layer on the baking sheet. Bake on the middle rack for 10 to 12 minutes, or until crispy and slightly brown.

PER SERVING: 162 Calories; 11g Fat; 6g Protein; 13g Carbohydrate; 5g Dietary Fiber; 8g Net Carbs

BUFFALO CHICKEN TENDERS

For many of you, your first instinct may be to walk away when you see pork rinds listed as an ingredient. Trust me when I tell you that you cannot taste them at all. Combining the pork rinds with the Parmesan cheese and the seasoning makes a perfectly crunchy breading that you can't tell apart from its gluten-filled, floury counterpart.

SERVES: 3-4

2 cups (105 g) crushed pork rinds

¾ cup (75 g) Parmesan cheese, finely grated

1 tsp garlic powder

1 tsp Italian seasoning

1 tsp onion powder

2 large eggs

1½ lbs (680 g) boneless skinless chicken breasts, cut into tender-size pieces

Cooking oil, for frying

¼ cup (60 g) butter (½ stick)

1 cup (240 ml) buffalo wing sauce

Combine the pork rinds, Parmesan cheese, garlic powder, Italian seasoning and onion powder in a food processor and give a few quick pulses. Pour the mixture into a thin layer on a large plate.

Crack the eggs into a shallow bowl and fork whisk. Dip the chicken tenders in the egg wash, and then dredge them in the breading mixture. Make sure both sides are thoroughly coated in the breading mixture.

Heat 1 to 2 inches (2.5 to 5 cm) of oil in a high-sided skillet. Once the oil is hot and begins to bubble slightly, drop the breaded chicken tenders into the oil. Fry until they are golden brown and crispy on both sides, about 3 minutes each side.

Remove the chicken tenders from the oil and place them on paper towels to absorb the excess grease.

In a sauce pan, over low heat, melt the butter and stir in the buffalo wing sauce. Heat until combined and warmed, about 5 minutes.

Lightly toss the chicken in the buffalo wing sauce.

PER SERVING: 335 Calories; 21g Fat; 33g Protein; 3g Carbohydrate; trace Dietary Fiber; 3g Net Carbs

A FEW NOTES ABOUT THIS RECIPE: Instead of frying them, you can bake them on parchment paper at 375°F (191°C) for 15 to 20 minutes. For either method, be careful not to flip them too many times as this will cause the breading to fall off. There are a couple of ways I like to make these—tossed in Sweet and Tangy Bacon Barbecue Sauce (page 182) or tossed in a fifty-fifty mixture of the barbecue sauce and the buffalo wing sauce.

SPICY BEEF QUESO DIP

We have all been at a party or gathering of some sort where there is a bowl of highly processed orange goo, masquerading as a cheese dip. We have all seen it, eaten it and probably even liked it even though we would hate to admit it. This is a version you will be proud to admit you ate. I will let you in on a little secret: If you add the juices from the tomatoes and green chiles and increase the heavy cream to a full cup (120 ml), this dip turns into a dynamite soup.

SERVES: 20

---

1 tbsp (8 g) chili powder

2 tsp (4 g) ground cumin

1 tsp onion powder

1 tsp celery salt

1 tbsp (15 ml) olive oil

8 oz (230 g) ground beef

½ cup (120 ml) heavy cream

2 (10 oz [285 g]) cans diced tomatoes and green chiles, juices drained

½ cup (60 g) sour cream

2 tbsp (35 g) horseradish Dijon mustard

3 cups (340 g) sharp cheddar cheese, shredded

Combine the chili powder, cumin, onion powder and celery salt in a small bowl.

In a skillet over medium-high heat, heat the olive oil and add the ground beef. Mix in the seasonings. Cook until the ground beef is browned. Drain any excess grease.

In a large saucepot over medium heat, combine the heavy cream and tomatoes with green chiles. Bring to a boil and then reduce the heat to low.

Mix in the sour cream and horseradish Dijon. Add the cheese and stir until it is melted and mixed in. Add the ground beef to the mixture. Let simmer, stirring occasionally, for 10 minutes.

PER SERVING: 144 Calories; 12g Fat; 7g Protein; 2g Carbohydrate; trace Dietary Fiber; 2g Net Carbs

CARAMELIZED ONION AND HORSERADISH DEVILED EGGS

Deviled eggs are making a big comeback and in a gourmet fashion. They are a timeless classic. They have graced the plastic tablecloths of barbecues, picnics and potlucks galore for decades and are usually one of the first empty plates. In this variation the mild sweetness of the caramelized onion, paired with the saltiness of the bacon and the subtle spiciness of the horseradish Dijon, makes for an abundance of flavor that will make you question everything you thought you knew about deviled eggs.

SERVES: 6

6 large eggs

1 tbsp (15 g) butter

1 tbsp (15 ml) olive oil

⅓ cup (50 g) onion, finely chopped

2 cloves garlic, minced

4 strips bacon, cooked crisp and crumbled

¼ cup (55 g) mayonnaise

1 tbsp (15 g) horseradish Dijon mustard

Hard boil the eggs. This is how I make perfect hard-boiled eggs: Place the eggs in a large saucepan. Add enough cold water that the eggs are fully submerged. Over high heat, bring water to a rolling boil. Once the water is boiling, remove the pan from the heat, cover and let sit for 12 minutes.

While the eggs are cooking, heat a medium sauté pan over medium-low heat. In the pan, heat the butter and olive oil, then add the onion and garlic. Sauté until the onion is nice and caramelized, about 20 minutes.

Cool the cooked eggs under cold water. Peel the eggs and slice in half lengthwise. Remove the yolks (reserving the whites separately) and fork mash them in a medium mixing bowl. To the bowl, add the caramelized onion and garlic, bacon, mayonnaise and horseradish Dijon. Mix until all the ingredients are well incorporated.

Put the mixture into a plastic bag. Squeeze the mixture to one corner of the bag and snip off the corner. Use this to pipe the mixture into the egg halves.

PER SERVING: 208 Calories; 19g Fat; 8g Protein; 2g Carbohydrate; trace Dietary Fiber; 2g Net Carbs

CAJUN CRAB CAKES

Crab cakes are one of those appetizers that my eyes naturally gravitate toward on a menu. However, it can be hard to find gluten-free crab cakes on a restaurant menu. Many of them contain bread crumbs, panko or something of the sort as a binding agent. In this recipe I took care of that problem and used crushed pork rinds to hold it all together. You can't taste them, and they play the part of bread crumbs perfectly. Now I can have my crab cakes and eat them, too! I love to serve these crab cakes with Russian Dressing (page 179).

SERVES: 4

2 tbsp (30 g) butter

1 large rib celery, chopped

½ cup (75 g) mixed bell pepper, chopped

1 shallot, chopped

2 cloves garlic, minced

Sea salt and black pepper, to taste

1 large egg

2 tbsp (30 g) mayonnaise

1 tbsp (15 ml) gluten-free Worcestershire sauce

1 tsp gluten-free spicy brown mustard

1 tsp hot sauce

½ cup (50 g) Parmesan cheese, grated

½ cup (30 g) crushed pork rinds

1 lb (455 g) crab meat, picked clean of shells

2 tbsp (30 ml) olive oil

Heat a large sauté pan over medium heat. In the pan, melt the butter, then add the celery, bell pepper, shallot, garlic, sea salt and black pepper. Sauté until the vegetables are translucent and soft, about 10 minutes.

In a large mixing bowl, combine the egg, mayonnaise, Worcestershire, spicy brown mustard and hot sauce. Add the sautéed vegetables and mix until all the ingredients are well incorporated. Mix in the Parmesan cheese and pork rinds. Fold the crab into the mixture.

Line a large plate or rimmed baking sheet with parchment or waxed paper. Form the crab mixture into 8 equal-size patties. Place the patties on the prepared baking sheet and refrigerate for 1 to 2 hours.

Panfry in olive oil in a large skillet over medium-high heat, until the crab cakes are golden brown and crispy on each side. Be careful not to flip them too many times or they will fall apart.

PER SERVING: 412 Calories; 28g Fat; 35g Protein; 4g Carbohydrate; 1g Dietary Fiber; 3g Net Carbs

TIP: This recipe yields 8 fairly large, entrée-size patties. If you make smaller patties, you could easily get 16 out of this recipe.

SMOKED SALMON BITES WITH HERBED CREAM CHEESE

The crunch of the cucumber in this recipe is a great replacement for a crispy cracker or crostini. I like to make a double batch of the herbed cream cheese and eat it as a snack with sugar snap peas, mini bell peppers and celery.

SERVES: 4

1 large cucumber

4 oz (115 g) cream cheese, softened

½ tsp minced onion flakes

½ tsp dried chives

¼ tsp dried parsley

¼ tsp dried dill

¼ tsp garlic powder

4 oz (155 g) smoked salmon or lox

2 tbsp (20 g) capers

Chopped dill, for garnish

Lemon slices, for serving

Slice the cucumber in ¼ to ½ inch (6 mm to 1.3 cm)-thick slices. This should yield about 20 slices.

In a medium mixing bowl, combine the cream cheese, onion flakes, chives, parsley, dill and garlic powder. Mix until all the ingredients are well incorporated.

Top each cucumber slice with the cream cheese mixture. Then top each piece with smoked salmon.

Sprinkle the capers over the top. Serve with a little chopped dill sprinkled over the top and fresh lemon slices on the side.

PER SERVING: 158 Calories; 12g Fat; 10g Protein; 3g Carbohydrate; 1g Dietary Fiber; 2g Net Carbs

3 MAIN DISHES

This chapter is where all your favorite comfort foods really start to transform before your eyes. I'm sure you have had plenty of Reuben sandwiches over the course of your lifetime, but have you ever had Reuben Stuffed Sweet Potatoes (page 75)? Who needs a bun for a chili dog when you can use the hot dog as a bun (page 68)? I've taken many of the traditional comfort foods that we have all come to know and love and transformed them into creative and easy-to-prepare, low-carb versions. Whether it is breakfast, lunch or dinner, this chapter has you covered.

Comfort foods are often tied to fond childhood memories and can make you feel nostalgic for simpler times. Whether that memory is of cooking in the kitchen with your grandmother, a favorite treat at a roadside food stand on a summer road trip or the first dish you ever learned to cook for yourself, this chapter is guaranteed to have at least one recipe that will transport you back to that time and place. My hope is that these recipes leave you with a full belly and a warm heart.

CARAMELIZED ONION AND PROSCIUTTO "MAC" AND CHEESE

I have never met a mac and cheese that I didn't like. Even bad mac and cheese still tastes good to me. Naturally, my love of this comfort food, popular among children and adults alike, was one of the hardest things to give up when switching over to a primal low-carb lifestyle. So, I set out to create a gourmet, low-carb version of one of my all-time favorite foods—this version, made with cauliflower and three cheeses, just so happens to be my favorite recipe in this entire book!

SERVES: 6

1 large head cauliflower, cleaned and trimmed, but left whole

2 tbsp (30 ml) olive oil

¼ cup (60 g) butter (½ stick), divided

1 medium onion, diced

3 cloves garlic, minced

1 cup (240 ml) heavy cream

½ cup (50 g) Parmesan cheese, grated

1 cup (115 g) sharp cheddar cheese, shredded

¼ cup (35 g) goat cheese

¼ tsp black pepper

6 oz (170 g) prosciutto, diced and cooked crisp

Preheat the oven to 350°F (177°C).

In a large, covered pot, filled with 1 inch (2.5 cm) of water, steam the cauliflower over high heat until fork tender, about 15 minutes. Remove from the heat, drain the water and allow the cauliflower to remain in the hot pot to draw out any excess moisture. This part is very important. You don't want to end up with mac and cheese soup.

Place the cauliflower in an 8 x 8-inch (20 x 20-cm) casserole dish. Using a fork, slightly mash the cauliflower to break it all apart.

In a large sauté pan over medium heat, heat the olive oil and 2 tablespoons (30 g) of the butter. Once the butter is melted, add the onion to the pan and sauté until nice and caramelized, about 20 minutes. Remove the caramelized onion from the pan and set aside.

To the same pan, add remaining 2 tablespoons (30 g) of butter and garlic. Sauté until the butter is melted and the garlic is fragrant. Add the heavy cream and Parmesan cheese. Stir continuously until the Parmesan is melted and the sauce begins to come to a boil. Mix in the cheddar cheese, goat cheese and black pepper. Stir until the cheeses are melted and well incorporated into the sauce. Reduce the heat to low and allow the sauce to thicken as it simmers, about 5 minutes.

Pour the cheese sauce evenly over top of the cauliflower. Layer the caramelized onion on top of the sauce. Lastly, layer the crispy prosciutto on top of the onion. Sprinkle with any leftover cheese you may have. Bake for 15 minutes.

PER SERVING: 461 Calories; 41g Fat; 19g Protein; 5g Carbohydrate; 1g Dietary Fiber; 4g Net Carbs

CHICKEN-FRIED STEAK WITH COUNTRY SAUSAGE GRAVY

Chicken-fried steak is my husband's absolute favorite breakfast. He orders it nearly every time we go out to eat. I was always confused by it. As he was eating it, I would ask him such questions as, "Why is it called chicken when it is actually beef?" and "Why do some places call it country fried steak and some call it chicken-fried steak?" "Are they just trying to confuse people?" Some deep conversation we had over breakfast. It all boils down to one answer: "Who cares? It's delicious!" Indeed, it is. Not only is chicken-fried steak delicious, it is a classic comfort food. I knew that I had to create a primal low-carb version of it.

SERVES: 4

---

1 lb (455 g) cube steak, 4 pieces pounded ¼ inch (6 mm) thick

Sea salt and black pepper

¼ cup (60 ml) heavy cream

2 large eggs

1½ cups (80 g) crushed pork rinds

½ cup (50 g) Parmesan cheese, grated

1½ tsp (4 g) onion powder

1½ tsp (5 g) garlic powder

1 tsp paprika

Pinch of cayenne pepper

Cooking oil

Country Sausage Gravy (page 157)

Sprinkle the cube steaks with sea salt and black pepper on both sides.

In a shallow bowl, combine the heavy cream and eggs. Fork whisk.

Combine the pork rinds, Parmesan cheese, onion powder, garlic powder, paprika and cayenne pepper. Pour the mixture into a thin layer on a large plate. This will be your breading.

In a large cast-iron skillet over medium-high heat, heat ¼ to ½ inch (6 mm to 1.3 cm) of oil.

Dip the cube steak into the egg wash and then dredge in the "breading," coating thoroughly on both sides.

Drop the breaded cube steak into the oil. Fry until crispy and golden brown, about 3 minutes for each side.

Top with the Country Sausage Gravy.

PER SERVING: 676 Calories; 51g Fat; 47g Protein; 5g Carbohydrate; trace Dietary Fiber; 5g Net Carbs

BLOODY MARY BURGERS

Your favorite Sunday morning hangover remedy just became your favorite burger. It's got all the staple ingredients, from tomato and Worcestershire sauce to olives and celery—well, all the staples minus the vodka.

SERVES: 4

1½ lbs (680 g) ground beef

2 tbsp (35 g) organic tomato paste

1 tbsp (15 ml) gluten-free Worcestershire sauce

3 cloves garlic, minced

1 tbsp (4 g) fresh parsley, chopped

1 tsp celery salt

½ tsp black pepper, or more to taste

1 medium tomato, chopped

4 large Spanish queen green olives, sliced

2 tbsp (30 ml) olive oil

2 ribs celery, diced

½ cup (75 g) onion, diced

Sea salt, to taste

4 large leaves iceberg lettuce

¼ cup (60 g) Creamy Horseradish Sauce (page 189)

4 pepperoncinis, for garnish (optional)

4 green olives, for garnish (optional)

In a large mixing bowl, combine the ground beef, tomato paste, Worcestershire sauce, garlic, parsley, celery salt and ½ teaspoon of black pepper. Mix until all the ingredients are well incorporated. Form into 4 equal-size patties. When forming your patties, press down in the center to make a reservoir. Doing this will make for even cooking as the burgers plump.

In a separate bowl, combine the tomatoes and sliced green olives.

In a large skillet over medium heat, heat the olive oil. Add the celery, onion and sea salt. Sauté until crisp-tender and translucent, about 4 minutes. Transfer the mixture to the bowl with the tomatoes and olives. Toss to combine the ingredients.

Increase the heat to medium-high and place the patties in the skillet. Cook until the burgers have developed a nice crust on the outside and have reached the desired level of doneness.

Place each burger patty on top of a lettuce leaf. Smear 1 tablespoon (15 g) of Creamy Horseradish Sauce over top of each burger.

Top each burger with a heaping portion of the vegetable mixture. Garnish with pepperoncinis and whole green olives, if desired.

PER SERVING: 639 Calories; 54g Fat; 30g Protein; 8g Carbohydrate; 2g Dietary Fiber; 6g Net Carbs

SHEPHERD'S PIE

There is something so warm and inviting about a shepherd's pie, fresh out of the oven. Traditionally, shepherd's pie would be topped with mashed potatoes, but this low-carb variation is topped with my Sour Cream and Onion Cauliflower Mash (page 144). It is an excellent substitution and is arguably just as good as the real thing, if not even better. I chose to make this in 6 individual single-serving ramekins. Alternatively, this can be done as one large casserole.

SERVES: 6

2 tbsp (60 g) butter

2 tbsp (60 ml) olive oil

1 cup (150 g) onion, diced

3 cloves garlic, minced

1 lb (455 g) ground beef

8 oz (230 g) ground pork

2 tbsp (35 g) organic tomato paste

2 tbsp (30 ml) gluten-free Worcestershire sauce

1 tsp dried oregano

Sea salt and black pepper, to taste

½ cup (65 g) carrot, chopped

½ cup (70 g) frozen peas

½ cup (75 g) red bell pepper, chopped

¾ cup (85 g) sharp Cheddar cheese, shredded

2 cups (300 g) Sour Cream and Onion Cauliflower Mash (page 144)

In a large skillet over medium-low heat, heat the butter and olive oil. Add the onion and garlic. Cook until the onion is translucent and the garlic is fragrant.

Add the ground beef and ground pork. Cook until the meats are browned and drain any excess grease. Add the tomato paste, Worcestershire sauce, oregano, sea salt and black pepper. Sauté for 5 minutes.

Add the carrots, peas and bell pepper. Mix them in and sauté for 10 minutes.

Preheat the oven to 375°F (190°C).

Divide the meat mixture evenly among 6 large ramekins. Top each ramekin with a layer of cheddar cheese.

Spoon the cauliflower mash into a plastic bag. Snip off the corner and pipe a thick layer of the cauliflower mash on top of the cheese layer.

Place the ramekins on a rimmed baking sheet and bake for 10 to 15 minutes, or until the top is lightly browned.

PER SERVING: 671 Calories; 58g Fat; 27g Protein; 10g Carbohydrate; 2g Dietary Fiber; 8g Net Carbs

CHICKEN FRIED "RICE" WITH BACON

Like a traditional chicken fried rice recipe, this version has chicken, carrots and peas, but is made primal and low-carb with the use of less traditional ingredients, such as cauliflower rice, coconut aminos and bacon. I am continuously in awe of how cauliflower can successfully masquerade as so many different foods. This recipe is no exception. It is definitely a primal low-carb staple. Would you believe me if I told you that just a few short years ago, I didn't like cauliflower? Now I can't imagine a weekly menu without it.

SERVES: 8

1 medium head cauliflower (about 1½ lbs [680 g])

¼ cup (60 g) butter (½ stick), divided

2 large green onions, chopped, whites and greens separated

3 cloves garlic, minced

¾ cup (100 g) carrot, thinly sliced on a bias

½ cup (75 g) yellow bell pepper, diced

½ cup (75 g) red bell pepper, diced

4 tbsp (60 ml) coconut aminos

1 tbsp (15 ml) sesame oil

1 tsp sea salt

½ tsp red pepper flakes

10 oz (285 g) chicken, cooked and chopped

6 slices thick-cut bacon, cooked crisp and crumbled

¾ cup (120 g) frozen peas

3 large eggs

Using a food processor or a box grater, rice the cauliflower.

Heat a wok over medium heat. In the wok, melt 1 tablespoon (15 g) of butter, then add the white portion of the green onions and the garlic. Sauté for 2 to 3 minutes.

Add the remaining 3 tablespoons (45 g) of butter, and the carrot and bell peppers, and sauté for 5 to 7 minutes.

Add the riced cauliflower, coconut aminos, sesame oil, sea salt and red pepper flakes. Stir-fry for 10 minutes. Mix in the chicken, bacon and peas. Stir-fry for an additional 5 minutes.

Crack the eggs into a bowl and fork whisk.

Push all the ingredients in the wok over to one side of the pan. Pour the eggs into the empty side of the pan and lightly scramble them. As the eggs begin to scramble, slowly mix them in with the rest of the dish.

Garnish with the green portion of the onions before serving.

PER SERVING: 259 Calories; 19g Fat; 13g Protein; 11g Carbohydrate; 4g Dietary Fiber; 7g Net Carbs

BEEF STROGANOFF MEATBALLS

The sour cream and mushroom base of this sauce is rich and decadent. To save myself time and make this an easy weeknight meal, I usually keep a batch of the precooked meatballs in the freezer. Then, all I have to do is make the sauce and dinner is served. This is another great dish to pair with the Sour Cream and Onion Cauliflower Mash (page 144).

SERVES: 4

2 lbs (910 g) ground beef

3 tbsp (15 g) fresh parsley, chopped

3 tbsp (45 ml) gluten-free Worcestershire sauce

4 cloves garlic, minced, divided

1½ tsp (4 g) onion powder

1½ tsp (5 g) garlic powder

1 tsp sea salt

1 tsp black pepper

2 tbsp (30 g) butter

2 tbsp (30 ml) olive oil

2 tbsp (30 ml) cooking sherry

1 small onion, diced

6 oz (170 g) cremini mushrooms, sliced

1 cup (240 ml) beef stock

2 tbsp (8 g) organic, gluten-free beef bouillon granules

¾ cup (90 g) sour cream

¼ cup (60 ml) heavy cream

In a large mixing bowl, combine the ground beef, parsley, Worcestershire sauce, half of the garlic, onion powder, garlic powder, sea salt and black pepper.

Once the mixture is well incorporated, form into meatballs. You should be able to get about 20 decently-sized meatballs from this mixture.

In a large sauté pan over medium-high heat, sear the meatballs, browning all over. Once the meatballs are cooked all the way through, remove them from the pan and set them aside.

To the same pan, add the butter, olive oil and cooking sherry. Reduce the heat to medium-low and add the onion, mushrooms and the remainder of the garlic. Sauté until the onion is caramelized and the mushrooms are tender and have released their liquid.

Deglaze the pan with the beef stock. Use a rubber spatula to scrape off and mix in any bits of onion and garlic stuck to the bottom of the pan. Add the beef bouillon granules and stir until dissolved.

Stir the sour cream and heavy cream into the sauce. Add the meatballs to the sauce and let the entire dish simmer, uncovered, over low heat for 10 minutes. Garnish the meatballs with any extra parsley before serving.

PER SERVING: 984 Calories; 84g Fat; 42g Protein; 13g Carbohydrate; 1g Dietary Fiber; 12g Net Carbs

BALSAMIC PEPPER STEAK KEBABS

The great thing about this recipe, other than the outstanding flavor, is that you can use any of your favorite vegetables and your favorite cut of meat. You can even use chicken, pork or shrimp in place of the steak. Get creative with things and have a "choose your own" kebab bar.

SERVES: 4

2 lbs (910 g) steak, cut into large chunks

1 large red bell pepper, cut into large chunks

1 large green bell pepper, cut into large chunks

1 large zucchini, sliced into ½ inch (1.3 cm)-thick slices

1 large summer squash, sliced into ½ inch (1.3 cm)-thick slices

1 small red onion, cut into large chunks

1 small sweet potato, halved lengthwise and sliced into ½ inch (1.3 cm)-thick slices

10 large button mushrooms, halved

2 cups (480 ml) Balsamic Vinaigrette (page 194)

Generous amount of cracked black pepper

In a large mixing bowl, combine the steak, bell peppers, zucchini, summer squash, red onion, sweet potato, mushrooms, Balsamic Vinaigrette and cracked black pepper.

Toss until the meat and vegetables are all thoroughly coated. Refrigerate for 1 to 2 hours.

Alternately thread the beef and vegetables onto about 16 skewers. Grill until the meat has reached the desired level of doneness.

PER SERVING: 256 Calories; 21g Fat; 10g Protein; 8g Carbohydrate; 2g Dietary Fiber; 6g Net Carbs

NOTE: A few things to keep in mind:
- If using bamboo skewers, soak them in water for 1 hour prior to grilling so that they do not burn.
- The total carb count for this recipe will be lower than listed as you will not be eating all of the marinade. You can lower the total carb count even further by omitting the sweet potatoes.
- From time to time, I like to substitute cauliflower for the sweet potatoes.
- Marinate the beef and vegetables for up to 24 hours for maximum flavor.

DECONSTRUCTED CABBAGE ROLLS

I have officially unstuffed the cabbage roll. This recipe takes a fairly labor-intensive classic and turns it into an easy weeknight dinner. With none of the fuss but all the flavor, this is another terrific make-ahead meal as the yield is large and it reheats well.

SERVES: 10

2 tbsp (30 g) butter

2 tbsp (30 ml) olive oil

1 cup (150 g) onion, diced

3 cloves garlic, minced

1½ lbs (680 g) ground beef

½ lb (230 g) ground pork

½ cup (120 ml) beef stock

2 tsp (10 g) sea salt

1 tsp paprika

1 tsp garlic powder

1 tsp onion powder

2 tsp (4 g) dried oregano

½ tsp dried thyme

1 tsp black pepper

2 (15 oz [425 g]) cans organic diced tomatoes, drained

1 (6 oz [170 g]) can organic tomato paste

2 tbsp (8 g) fresh parsley, chopped

1 medium head cabbage, halved and sliced

2 cups (240 g) riced cauliflower

In a large skillet or wok over medium heat, heat the butter and olive oil. Add the onion and garlic. Cook until the onion is translucent and garlic is fragrant.

Add the ground beef and ground pork to the pan. Cook until browned and drain any excess grease. Add the beef stock, sea salt, paprika, garlic powder, onion powder, oregano, thyme and black pepper. Simmer for 5 minutes.

Add the tomatoes, tomato paste and parsley and mix in. Next, mix in the cabbage and riced cauliflower. Reduce the heat to low and simmer for 20 minutes.

PER SERVING: 369 Calories; 29g Fat; 18g Protein; 11g Carbohydrate; 3g Dietary Fiber; 8g Net Carbs

ITALIAN MEATBALLS WITH TOMATO CREAM SAUCE

Who doesn't love meatballs? I like to start with this recipe as a base and get creative with it from there. One of my favorite variations is to finely chop a handful of mixed bell peppers, sun-dried tomatoes and mushrooms and throw them into the mixture. It adds a lot of extra flavor and is another great way to sneak in more vegetables.

SERVES: 4

1½ lbs (680 g) ground beef

½ lb (230 g) ground pork

½ cup (50 g) Parmesan cheese, finely grated

4 cloves garlic, minced

1 large egg

4 tbsp (15 g) fresh parsley, chopped

2 tsp (10 g) sea salt

2 tsp (5 g) onion powder

1½ tsp (3 g) Italian seasoning

1½ tsp (3 g) dried oregano

¾ tsp black pepper

1 cup (240 ml) Tomato Cream Sauce (page 186)

Parsley, to garnish

Preheat the oven to 350°F (177°C).

In a large mixing bowl, combine the ground beef, ground pork, Parmesan cheese, garlic, egg, parsley, sea salt, onion powder, Italian seasoning, oregano and black pepper. Mix until all the ingredients are well incorporated.

Form the mixture into 2-inch (5-cm) meatballs. Transfer to a rimmed baking sheet. Bake for 20 minutes.

Top the meatballs with the Tomato Cream Sauce and garnish with any leftover chopped parsley.

PER SERVING: 819 Calories; 66g Fat; 47g Protein; 9g Carbohydrate; 2g Dietary Fiber; 7g Net Carbs

NOTE: You can also pan cook these meatballs in a hot cast-iron skillet over medium-high heat using your favorite cooking oil. My favorite is avocado.

STUFFED FLAT IRON PINWHEELS

Making steak pinwheels is a great way to utilize and jazz up less-expensive cuts of meat. You can make these with a flat iron, flank or skirt steak. The sun-dried tomatoes, feta and garlic pack a ton of fresh flavor into this recipe.

SERVES: 4

1½ lbs (680 g) flat iron steak

Sea salt and black pepper

1 cup (30 g) packed fresh spinach leaves

1 cup (60 g) sun-dried tomatoes

¾ cup (115 g) feta cheese, crumbled

3 cloves garlic, thinly sliced

Preheat the oven to broil at 500°F (260°C).

Butterfly the flat iron steak. Open the meat so that it lies flat. Wrap the meat with plastic wrap and pound with a meat mallet to flatten to a ¼-inch (6-mm) thickness.

Sprinkle the meat with sea salt and black pepper on both sides. Evenly layer on the spinach, sun-dried tomatoes, feta cheese and garlic. Roll up tightly and tie with cooking twine. Alternatively, you can use presoaked bamboo skewers to hold the roll together, placing a skewer every 2 inches (5 cm).

Slice into 8 equal slices. Transfer the pinwheels to a baking sheet. Broil on high heat for 4 to 5 minutes, or until the meat has reached the desired level of doneness.

PER SERVING: 419 Calories; 24g Fat; 39g Protein; 10g Carbohydrate; 2g Dietary Fiber; 8g Net Carbs

MUFFULETTA CHICKEN

As I mentioned in the Olive Salad recipe (page 25), I love muffuletta. It is my all-time favorite New Orleans classic. I make my way to "The Big Easy" once every couple of years or so, and getting a muffuletta is always close to the top of my list! This muffuletta chicken is a way for me to get a taste of New Orleans from home. By skipping the bread and turning it into a chicken dish, I can indulge in the rich, deliciousness of muffuletta anytime I want, in a version that fits my primal low-carb lifestyle.

SERVES: 4

1½ lbs (680 g) chicken breasts (4 breasts total)

¼ cup (60 g) butter (½ stick)

4 oz (115 g) gluten-free salami, thinly sliced

4 oz (115 g) provolone cheese, sliced

4 oz (115 g) mortadella, thinly sliced

4 oz (115 g) mozzarella cheese, sliced

4 oz (115 g) capocollo, thinly sliced

2 cups (270 g) Olive Salad (page 25)

In a large skillet over medium-high heat, pan-sear the chicken breasts in butter until they are golden brown and slightly crispy, about 8 minutes each side.

Preheat the oven to 350°F (177°C).

Place the chicken breasts on a rimmed baking sheet. Layer each breast with salami, provolone, mortadella, mozzarella and capocollo. Bake on the middle rack for 10 minutes.

Remove the chicken breasts from the oven and top with a heaping portion of Olive Salad.

PER SERVING: 846 Calories; 64g Fat; 57g Protein; 7g Carbohydrate; 1g Dietary Fiber; 6g Net Carbs

MEXICAN SPAGHETTI SQUASH TACO BAKE

Spice up your taco Tuesdays with a casserole the whole family will love. Using a base of spaghetti squash eliminates the need for starchy taco shells, making this dish low-carb, while still satisfying your taco craving. In our house, we like to top this with sour cream and sliced fresh avocado.

SERVES: 6

1 medium spaghetti squash

1 tbsp (15 ml) olive oil

6 tbsp (55 g) Taco Seasoning (page 15), divided

1 lb (455 g) ground beef

⅔ cup (160 ml) water

1 (10 oz [285 g]) can diced tomatoes and green chiles

1 cup (115 g) sharp cheddar cheese, shredded

10 black olives, sliced

10 pickled jalapeño slices

2 green onions, chopped, for garnish

Preheat the oven to 400°F (205°C). Line a rimmed baking sheet with parchment paper.

Halve the spaghetti squash lengthwise; scrape out and discard the seeds. Place the squash halves, cut side up, on the baking sheet. Brush both halves with olive oil and sprinkle 1 tablespoon (9 g) of the taco seasoning over the top. Bake for 45 minutes.

While the spaghetti squash is baking, brown the ground beef in a medium skillet over medium-high heat. Drain any excess grease from the pan. Add the water and the remaining taco seasoning to the pan and mix in. Reduce the heat to low, simmer and let thicken.

Once the spaghetti squash has finished baking, remove it from the oven and use a fork to scrape the flesh out of the shell. Layer it in the bottom of a large casserole dish or pie pan.

On top of the spaghetti squash, layer on the taco meat. On top of the taco meat, layer on the diced tomatoes and green chiles. Cover the chiles with the cheddar cheese. Top the cheese with the olives and jalapeños.

Reduce the oven temperature to 350°F (177°C). Bake the casserole for 20 minutes. Remove from the oven and top with the green onions.

PER SERVING: 387 Calories; 31g Fat; 19g Protein; 9g Carbohydrate; 2g Dietary Fiber; 7g Net Carbs

CHILI DOGS

Chili dogs are a summer cookout must! Sunny weather always makes me think of backyard grilling, and when I was growing up, backyard grilling always included hot dogs. Although certain foods are so reminiscent of a particular season, I am a firm believer that good food should be eaten year-round. I love to butterfly open the hot dogs and fry them in butter. Who needs a starchy bun, when you can use a hot dog as the bun? These chili dogs are spectacular topped with a dollop of sour cream and some chopped green onions.

SERVES: 4

8 grass-fed, all-beef hot dogs

2 tbsp (30 g) butter

2 cups (500 g) Three-Meat No-Bean Chili (page 100)

1 cup (115 g) sharp cheddar cheese, shredded

1/3 cup (50 g) onion, diced

Sour cream, for garnish (optional)

Green onions, for garnish (optional)

Slice the hot dogs in half lengthwise, not cutting all the way through. Butterfly the hot dogs open. In a large skillet over medium-high heat, melt the butter. When the butter starts to brown, add the hot dogs to the pan, cut side down. Fry on both sides until heated all the way through and slightly crispy.

Plate the hot dogs and top with the chili, cheddar cheese and onion. Garnish with sour cream and green onions, if desired.

PER SERVING: 682 Calories; 58g Fat; 30g Protein; 9g Carbohydrate; 2g Dietary Fiber; 7g Net Carbs

SLOW COOKER PULLED PORK WITH BACON BARBECUE SAUCE

I love when a dish is simple to make, yet incredibly flavorful. It doesn't get much easier than this. The slow cooker does all the work for you. I like to serve this over top of a bed of the Zesty Coleslaw (page 143).

SERVES: 10

Large red onion, cut into large chunks

4 garlic cloves

2 large ribs celery, cut into sticks

2 cups (480 ml) beef stock

5 lbs (2¼ kg) pork roast

Sea salt and black pepper

4 cups (920 g) Sweet and Tangy Bacon Barbecue Sauce (page 182)

Heat a large slow cooker on the high setting. In the slow cooker, combine the onion, garlic, celery and beef stock. Sprinkle the pork roast with a generous coating of sea salt and black pepper and place the roast in the slow cooker on top of the vegetables. Cover and cook for 7 hours.

After 7 hours, pull the pork roast out of the slow cooker and put it in a large bowl. Drain the liquid and discard the vegetables from the slow cooker. Fork shred the pork roast and place it back in the slow cooker. Pour the barbecue sauce over the pork and mix in. Cook for 1 additional hour.

PER SERVING (Does not include sauce): 388 Calories; 24g Fat; 35g Protein; 7g Carbohydrate; 1g Dietary Fiber; 6g Net Carbs

SUPREME PIZZA STUFFED PEPPERS

If you were to ask anyone, I bet they would list pizza as one of the top five comfort foods of all time. I am giving you back pizza! You can now feel free to eat pizza and not feel guilty about it. This recipe is also a great way to introduce your children to bell peppers and a variety of other fresh vegetables.

SERVES: 4

1 large red bell pepper, halved, ribs and seeds removed

1 large orange bell pepper, halved, ribs and seeds removed

1 large yellow bell pepper, halved, ribs and seeds removed

1 large green bell pepper, halved, ribs and seeds removed

1½ cups (170 g) mozzarella cheese, shredded, divided

1 cup (255 g) Easy Peasy Pizza Sauce (page 181)

2 oz (60 g) pepperoni slices

2 oz (60 g) Canadian bacon slices

4 button mushrooms, sliced

10 black olives, sliced

⅓ cup (50 g) onion, diced

½ cup (50 g) Parmesan cheese, grated

1 tbsp (6 g) Italian seasoning

Preheat the oven to 400°F (205°C). Line a rimmed baking sheet with parchment paper.

Line the peppers on the baking sheet and bake on the middle rack for 15 minutes. Remove the peppers from the oven and pour out any excess moisture.

Sprinkle 1 tablespoon (20 g) of the mozzarella into the bottom of each pepper cup. Top the mozzarella with 2 tablespoons (35 g) of the pizza sauce. Evenly divide the pepperoni, Canadian bacon, mushrooms, olives and onion among the 8 pepper cups.

Top each pepper cup with 2 tablespoons (35 g) of mozzarella cheese. Return the peppers to the oven and bake on the top rack for an additional 10 minutes. Remove the peppers from the oven and top each one with 1 tablespoon (5 g) of Parmesan cheese and a sprinkle of Italian seasoning. Return the peppers to the oven and broil for 5 minutes.

PER SERVING: 394 Calories; 24g Fat; 25g Protein; 24g Carbohydrate; 5g Dietary Fiber; 19g Net Carbs

REUBEN STUFFED SWEET POTATOES

Reuben sandwiches are classic diner fare. I challenge you to walk into any greasy-spoon diner and not immediately find a Reuben sandwich on their menu or specials board. The saltiness of the corned beef, combined with the sweetness of the Russian dressing and the acidity of the sauerkraut, is a flavor that I have never seen replicated in any other dish. I love to garnish this dish with some chopped green onions.

SERVES: 4

2 large sweet potatoes

¼ cup (60 g) butter (½ stick)

1 tsp onion powder

1 tsp caraway seeds

2 tbsp (60 ml) olive oil

1 lb (455 g) precooked deli style corned beef, chopped

1½ cups (215 g) sauerkraut

3 cloves garlic, minced

4 slices Swiss cheese

⅓ cup (80 g) Russian Dressing (page 179)

Chopped green onion, for garnish

Preheat the oven to 400°F (205°C). Line a rimmed baking sheet with parchment paper.

Halve the sweet potatoes lengthwise. Place cut side up on the baking sheet. Top each sweet potato half with 1 tablespoon (15 g) of the butter. Sprinkle with the onion powder and caraway seeds. Bake for 45 minutes to 1 hour.

While the sweet potatoes are baking, heat a large skillet over medium heat. Heat the olive oil in the pan, then add the corned beef, sauerkraut and garlic. Sauté until heated through, about 10 minutes. Drain any excess liquid and lower the heat to low.

When the sweet potatoes are finished baking, fork rake the top of them to loosen their flesh.

Top each sweet potato with a heaping portion of the corned beef mixture. Top with a slice of Swiss cheese and drizzle with Russian dressing. Garnish with chopped green onion, if desired.

PER SERVING: 1025 Calories; 79g Fat; 55g Protein; 24g Carbohydrate; 4g Dietary Fiber; 20g Net Carbs

OLD-FASHIONED MEAT LOAF

Whenever I make a meat loaf, it instantly takes me back to my childhood. We ate it at least once a week, and I was one of those kids that loved it. That love followed me into adulthood and I make it often for my own family. I have made several variations over the years, but this version is the one that gets requested the most. I think the reasoning for this is that my family can taste all the love I mix into it. That and the Dry Onion Soup Mix (page 15).

SERVES: 8

1½ lbs (680 g) ground beef

1 lb (455 g) ground pork sausage

3 cloves garlic, minced

2 large eggs

1 cup (55 g) crushed pork rinds

¼ cup (70 g) organic tomato paste

¼ cup (30 g) Dry Onion Soup Mix (page 15)

2 tbsp (30 ml) gluten-free Worcestershire sauce

Preheat the oven to 400°F (205°C).

In a large mixing bowl, combine the ground beef, pork sausage, garlic, eggs, pork rinds, tomato paste, onion soup mix and Worcestershire sauce. Mix until all the ingredients are well incorporated.

Transfer the mixture to a large loaf pan and bake for 45 minutes.

PER SERVING: 583 Calories; 49g Fat; 28g Protein; 6g Carbohydrate; 1g Dietary Fiber; 5g Net Carbs

EGGPLANT LASAGNA

This lasagna recipe replaces traditional strips of pasta noodles with slices of fresh eggplant, layered between rich layers of ricotta, Parmesan and mozzarella cheese and my special Hearty Meat Sauce (page 177).

SERVES: 8

1 large eggplant

2 tbsp (30 ml) olive oil

Sea salt and black pepper

2 cups (500 g) ricotta cheese

1 cup (100 g) Parmesan cheese, shredded

8 small fresh basil leaves, chopped

6 cups (1,500 ml) Hearty Meat Sauce (page 177)

2 cups (240 g) mozzarella cheese, shredded

1 tbsp (6 g) dried oregano

Preheat the oven to 400°F (205°C). Line a baking sheet with parchment paper.

Cut off the ends of the eggplant and slice lengthwise in ¼ inch (6 mm)-thick slices. You should end up with about 10 slices total. Brush each slice of eggplant with olive oil on both sides and sprinkle with a little sea salt and black pepper. Bake for about 7 minutes on each side.

In a large mixing bowl, combine the ricotta cheese, Parmesan cheese and basil. Mix until all the ingredients are well incorporated.

Pour 2 cups (500 ml) of the meat sauce into the bottom of an 8 x 13-inch (20 x 33-cm) baking dish. Spread into an even layer. On top of the sauce, layer half of the eggplant slices.

Layer half of the ricotta mixture on top of the eggplant, spreading evenly across the entire dish. Sprinkle ½ cup (60 g) of the mozzarella cheese on top of the ricotta mixture.

Pour 2 cups (500 ml) of the meat sauce on top of the cheese and spread in an even layer across the entire dish. Layer the remaining eggplant on top of the sauce.

Layer the second half of the ricotta mixture on top of the eggplant, spreading evenly across the entire dish. Sprinkle ½ cup (60 g) of the mozzarella cheese on top of the ricotta mixture.

Pour remaining 2 cups (500 ml) of the meat sauce on top of the cheese and spread in an even layer across the entire dish.

Sprinkle the remaining 1 cup (120 g) of mozzarella cheese evenly across the entire dish. Sprinkle the oregano on top of the cheese. Cover with foil and bake for 30 minutes. Remove the foil and broil on high for 5 to 8 minutes. Let stand for 15 minutes before cutting.

PER SERVING: 568 Calories; 43g Fat; 31g Protein; 16g Carbohydrate; 4g Dietary Fiber; 12g Net Carbs

SHRIMP SCAMPI

What's not to love about delicate shrimp swirling around in a rich pool of garlic and butter? If you are short on time and looking to throw together a meal that will taste as if you spent hours in the kitchen, then this is the dish for you. This recipe will have you in and out of the kitchen in about 15 minutes.

SERVES: 4

1½ lbs (680 g) jumbo shrimp, peeled and deveined

Sea salt and black pepper

¼ cup (60 g) butter (½ stick)

3 cloves garlic, minced

3 tbsp (45 ml) chicken stock

2 tbsp (30 ml) lemon juice

1 tbsp (6 g) lemon zest

1 tsp onion powder

2 tbsp (8 g) fresh parsley, chopped

½ tsp crushed red pepper flakes

Sprinkle the shrimp with sea salt and black pepper.

In a large skillet over medium heat, melt the butter. Once the butter has melted, add the garlic and sauté for about 1 minute. Be careful as garlic can burn and turn bitter very fast.

Add the chicken stock, lemon juice, lemon zest and onion powder. Let simmer for 2 to 3 minutes.

Add the shrimp and sauté, stirring often, until the shrimp have all turned pink, about 5 to 6 minutes.

Add the fresh parsley and red pepper flakes and toss before serving.

PER SERVING: 298 Calories; 15g Fat; 35g Protein; 4g Carbohydrate; trace Dietary Fiber; 4g Net Carbs

LEMON-GARLIC PORK STEAKS WITH MUSHROOMS

Don't let the simplicity of this dish fool you; thanks to the butter and the lemon pepper seasoning, it is packed full of flavor. One of my favorite things about this recipe is how versatile it is. I have made it using chicken in place of pork and it is equally delicious. From time to time I also like to add capers and artichoke hearts for an extra burst of flavor. When preparing this dish, if you do not have a large enough pan, you may need to cook the pork in batches.

SERVES: 4

4 large, bone-in pork steaks (about 2 lbs [910 g])

2 tsp (6 g) lemon pepper seasoning

1½ tsp (8 g) sea salt, or more to taste

3 tbsp (45 g) butter, divided

3 tbsp (45 ml) olive oil, divided

1 cup (240 ml) chicken stock, divided

6 cloves garlic, minced

8 oz (230 g) cremini mushrooms, quartered

1 lemon, thinly sliced

2 tbsp (8 g) fresh parsley, chopped

Season the pork steaks on both sides with lemon pepper seasoning and sea salt.

In a large skillet over medium-high heat, heat 2 tablespoons (30 g) of the butter and 2 tablespoons (30 ml) of the olive oil. Pan-sear the pork steaks until they are cooked all the way through and browned on both sides. Remove from the pan, cover and set aside.

Reduce the heat to medium and add the remaining 1 tablespoon (15 g) of butter and 1 tablespoon (15 ml) of olive oil to the pan. Deglaze the pan with ½ cup (120 ml) of the chicken stock. Use a rubber spatula to scrape any remaining bits of pork from the bottom of the pan and mix into the sauce.

Add the garlic and mushrooms to the pan. Sauté until the mushrooms are soft and the garlic is fragrant. Add the remaining ½ cup (120 ml) of the chicken stock, lemon slices and parsley to the pan. Let the sauce simmer for 5 minutes.

Return the pork steaks to the pan and sauté for an additional 5 to 10 minutes, while basting the steaks with the pan sauce.

PER SERVING: 483 Calories; 28g Fat; 50g Protein; 6g Carbohydrate; 1g Dietary Fiber; 5g Net Carbs

ZUCCHINI NOODLE PUTTANESCA WITH PRAWNS

Puttanesca was a regular on the menu at both of the Italian restaurants that I worked in. In Italian, *puttanesca* literally translates to "whore." That was always a fun story to explain to the guests that came in. A traditional puttanesca is a robust tomato sauce with light, fresh ingredients. It is typically briny and somewhat salty in nature and usually contains anchovies. I went a slightly less traditional route and made mine with prawns.

SERVES: 8

1 lb (455 g) prawns (jumbo shrimp), peeled and deveined

Sea salt and black pepper

2 tbsp (30 ml) olive oil

4 cloves garlic, minced

⅔ cup (100 g) onion, diced

1 (28 oz [795 g]) can organic stewed tomatoes

¼ cup (70 g) organic tomato paste

20 Kalamata olives, sliced

¼ cup (35 g) capers

3 tbsp (15 g) fresh parsley, chopped

½ tsp crushed red pepper flakes

4 medium zucchini, spiral sliced
(about 1½ lbs [680 g])

Sprinkle the pawns with sea salt and black pepper.

In a large saucepot over medium heat, heat the olive oil. Add the garlic and onion. Cook until the onion is translucent and the garlic is fragrant.

Add the stewed tomatoes to the pot and mash. Mix in the tomato paste, Kalamata olives, capers, parsley and crushed red pepper flakes. Bring to a boil over medium heat and then reduce the heat to low, to simmer.

Add the seasoned prawns and zucchini noodles to the sauce. Let simmer until the prawns are cooked and the zucchini noodles are tender. Taste and add additional salt and pepper if needed.

PER SERVING: 170 Calories; 7g Fat; 14g Protein; 13g Carbohydrate; 3g Dietary Fiber; 10g Net Carbs

HERBED BUTTER ROASTED CHICKEN

Roasting a chicken with butter produces the juiciest chicken you will ever sink your teeth into. Packing the butter and seasoning between the breasts and the skin locks in the flavor and keeps the chicken moist all throughout cooking.

SERVES: 4

6 tbsp (90 g) butter, at room temperature

2 tsp (3 g) dried thyme

2 tsp (2 g) rubbed sage

2 tsp (5 g) minced onion flakes

1 tsp sea salt

1 tsp garlic powder

½ tsp black pepper

4 lbs (2 kg) roasting chicken

1½ cups (355 ml) chicken stock

Preheat the oven to 400°F (205°C).

In a small bowl, combine the butter, thyme, sage, onion flakes, sea salt, garlic powder and black pepper. Mix until all the ingredients are well incorporated. If you have a tough time mixing these or did not have time to let your butter soften, you can mix these in a food processor or with a hand mixer.

Place the chicken, breast side up, in a shallow roasting pan. Add the chicken stock to the bottom of the roasting pan.

Gently loosen the skin covering the breasts of the chicken, lifting it away from the breast, creating a pocket between the breast and the skin.

Pack half of the herbed butter between the skin and the breasts, distributing it evenly. Rub the other half of the herbed butter all over the top of the chicken.

Bake on the middle rack for 30 minutes. Take the chicken out of the oven, baste the juices over the top of it and return it to the oven. Roast for an additional 30 to 45 minutes, basting every 10 minutes.

PER SERVING: 887 Calories; 70g Fat; 57g Protein; 3g Carbohydrate; 1g Dietary Fiber; 2g Net Carbs

COCONUT-CASHEW CRUSTED CHICKEN

For this recipe, instead of gluten-filled breading, I opted for a mix of crushed cashews, coconut flakes and coconut flour. The combo packs a sweet and salty punch and a mouthwatering crunch.

SERVES: 4

½ cup (110 g) coconut oil

1 cup (130 g) raw cashews

½ cup (40 g) unsweetened coconut flakes

¼ cup (30 g) coconut flour

Sea salt and black pepper, to taste

¼ cup (60 ml) coconut milk

1 large egg

1½ lbs (680 g) chicken breast, cut into tender-size pieces

Preheat the oven to 450°F (233°C). Scoop the coconut oil into a large cast-iron skillet. Place the skillet in the oven and heat until the coconut oil melts and starts to bubble.

Combine the cashews, coconut flakes, coconut flour, sea salt and black pepper in a food processor. Give a few quick pulses until all the ingredients are well combined. This will be your breading. Pour the mixture onto a large plate and spread into a thin, even layer.

In a shallow bowl, fork whisk the coconut milk and egg together.

Coat the chicken pieces in the breading, dip into the egg mixture and then coat generously in the breading again.

Place the breaded chicken tenders in the hot skillet. Return the skillet to the oven and cook for 25 to 30 minutes, carefully flipping halfway through.

PER SERVING: 776 Calories; 65g Fat; 38g Protein; 16g Carbohydrate; 5g Dietary Fiber; 11g Net Carbs

---

NOTE: Before breading the chicken, I highly recommend patting it dry first to get rid of any excess moisture. This will help your breading stay on. There are some easy substitutions you can do with this recipe based on the ingredients you have on hand. In place of the coconut flour, you can use almond flour. In place of the coconut milk, you can use almond milk or even heavy cream.

PORK AND CABBAGE STIR-FRY

This stir-fry is hearty and fresh, with a light but flavorful taste. I highly recommend prepping the pork and letting it marinate for 24 hours before cooking. This will make the pork even more tender and the dish will be a lot more flavorful.

SERVES: 6

1 lb (455 g) pork tenderloin, cut into ¼ inch (6 mm)-thick strips

1 tsp sea salt

½ tsp black pepper

2 tbsp (30 ml) olive oil

3 tbsp (45 ml) gluten-free soy sauce or coconut aminos, divided

2 tsp (10 ml) sesame oil

2 cloves garlic, minced

½ tsp crushed red pepper flakes

1 red bell pepper, julienned

½ cup (30 g) mushrooms, thinly sliced

1 small head of cabbage, shredded

2 tbsp (20 g) toasted sesame seeds, for garnish

2 green onions, chopped, for garnish

Season the pork strips with the sea salt and black pepper.

In a medium bowl, whisk together the olive oil, 2 tablespoons (30 ml) of the soy sauce, sesame oil, garlic and crushed red pepper flakes. Add the pork to the sauce and toss until it is well coated.

Heat a large wok over medium-high heat. Add the pork, including all the marinade, and the bell pepper and mushrooms. Stir-fry until the pork is cooked all the way through, 5 to 7 minutes.

Add the cabbage and remaining 1 tablespoon (15 ml) of soy sauce to the wok and continue to stir-fry until the cabbage is slightly wilted, 2 to 3 minutes. Garnish with sesame seeds and green onions and serve.

PER SERVING: 182 Calories; 10g Fat; 18g Protein; 4g Carbohydrate; 2g Dietary Fiber; 2g Net Carbs

CHILI-LIME SHRIMP AVOCADO BOATS

This is a light dish that makes for a perfect summer dinner outside. The tartness of freshly squeezed lime juice is the perfect counterbalance to the heat of the taco seasoning.

SERVES: 4

---

1 lb (455 g) medium shrimp, peeled and deveined

Juice of 1 lime

3 cloves garlic, minced

2 tbsp (30 ml) coconut aminos

1 tbsp (10 g) Taco Seasoning (page 15)

2 large avocados, halved, cored and cubed (save the skins)

1 small tomato, diced

½ cup (85 g) artichoke hearts, roughly chopped

⅓ cup (50 g) red onion, chopped

¼ cup (35 g) capers

2 tbsp (30 ml) olive oil

Sea salt and black pepper, to taste

In a large bowl, combine the shrimp, lime juice, garlic, coconut aminos and taco seasoning. Toss until the shrimp are thoroughly coated and set aside.

In a separate bowl, combine the cubed avocados, tomato, artichoke hearts, red onion and capers. Drizzle olive oil over avocado mixture and sprinkle with sea salt and black pepper.

In a medium sauté pan over medium heat, sauté the shrimp, including all the marinade, until the shrimp are pink and cooked through, about 3 to 5 minutes.

Mix the shrimp into the avocado mixture. Fill the avocado skins with heaping mounds of the mixture.

PER SERVING: 390 Calories; 25g Fat; 27g Protein; 19g Carbohydrate; 5g Dietary Fiber; 14g Net Carbs

---

SOUPS AND SALADS

I am a firm believer that you eat with your eyes first. You are naturally drawn to bright, bold colors and colorful food is just more craveable and satisfying. Have you ever looked at a plate of food and felt your mouth begin to water? I would venture to guess that the plate contained a wide spectrum of vibrant colors, and I'd be willing to bet that the Blackened Steak Salad (page 99) will produce a similar reaction.

These bursts of color are my favorite thing about salads. They are usually chock-full of colorful vegetables and sometimes even a variety of meats and cheeses. There is nothing quite like biting into a cold, fresh, crisp salad. The salads I have prepared for you in this book are great accompaniments to a wide variety of main courses, but they also hold their weight as a full meal all on their own. The Italian Chopped Salad (page 104) and Buffalo Chicken Wedge Salad (page 103) are especially satisfying.

The soups in this chapter, such as my favorite, Philly Cheesesteak Soup (page 108), are all prepared in a slow cooker. This makes for deeper, richer flavors, and there is the added benefit of letting the slow cooker do all the work for you while you sit back, relax and enjoy quality time with your family.

BACON CHEESEBURGER SOUP

A couple of things were uncertain to me as I set out to make this soup. One was whether it would even taste good, and two was whether I would be able to capture all the flavors of a bacon cheeseburger and not just the meat and the cheese. Well, I now have my answers. It turned out spectacular and has all the flavor components of a bacon cheeseburger. It is as if you can actually taste each individual condiment.

SERVES: 10

4 cups (950 ml) beef stock

4 cloves garlic, minced

1 medium tomato, diced

2 tbsp (35 g) gluten-free Dijon mustard

2 tbsp (30 ml) gluten-free Worcestershire sauce

2 tbsp (8 g) fresh parsley, chopped

1 tsp sea salt

½ tsp black pepper

1½ lbs (680 g) ground beef

1 small onion, diced

1 cup (115 g) cheddar cheese, shredded

1 cup (240 ml) heavy cream

1 lb (455 g) bacon, cooked crisp and crumbled

Additional cheddar cheese, for garnish (optional)

Additional tomatoes, for garnish (optional)

Heat a slow cooker on the low setting.

In the slow cooker, combine the beef stock, garlic, tomato, mustard, Worcestershire sauce, parsley, sea salt and black pepper.

In a large skillet over medium-high heat, cook the ground beef and onion until the beef is browned and the onion is soft and translucent. Drain any excess grease and add the beef and onion to the slow cooker. Cover and cook for 6 hours.

To the slow cooker, mix in the cheddar cheese, heavy cream and bacon crumbles. Cover and cook for 1 additional hour. Garnish to taste with additional cheddar cheese and tomatoes, if desired.

PER SERVING: 665 Calories; 53g Fat; 30g Protein; 13g Carbohydrate; 1g Dietary Fiber; 12g Net Carbs

BLACKENED STEAK SALAD

My husband says that this is about as manly as a salad can get. It is fresh, crisp, colorful and loaded with meat. My favorite thing about this salad is the wonderfully contrasting textures as you work your way through it.

SERVES: 4

1½ lbs (680 g) flat iron steak, sliced into ½ inch (1.3 cm)-thick strips

4 tbsp (60 ml) olive oil, divided

2 tsp (5 g) paprika

1½ tsp (5 g) garlic powder

1½ tsp (4 g) onion powder

1½ tsp (3 g) dried thyme

½ tsp cayenne pepper

½ tsp dried basil

½ tsp ground cumin

½ tsp celery salt

¼ tsp dried oregano

2 tbsp (30 g) butter

1 medium onion, thinly sliced

2 cloves garlic, minced

Sea salt and black pepper, to taste

4 large mushrooms, thinly sliced

1 large head romaine lettuce, shredded

2 cups (60 g) fresh spinach leaves, packed

1 cup (135 g) blue cheese crumbles

16 grape tomatoes, halved

1 medium orange bell pepper, sliced

1 medium yellow bell pepper, sliced

1 medium avocado, peeled, pitted and sliced

In a large mixing bowl, toss the steak strips in 2 tablespoons (30 ml) of olive oil. In a small mixing bowl, combine the paprika, garlic powder, onion powder, thyme, cayenne pepper, basil, cumin, celery salt and oregano. Sprinkle the seasoning over the top of the steak and toss in the bowl until all the meat is evenly coated. Set aside.

In a large sauté pan, heat the remaining 2 tablespoons (30 ml) of olive oil and the butter over medium-low heat. Add the onion, garlic, sea salt and black pepper. Sauté until the onion is a nice caramel color, about 20 minutes. Add the mushrooms and sauté until they are soft and have released their liquid, about 10 minutes.

While the onion is caramelizing, divide the romaine and spinach among 4 plates. Top each plate of lettuce with one quarter of the blue cheese crumbles, tomatoes, orange and yellow bell pepper and avocado. Line each topping in its own individual row.

Heat the oven on broil. Line up the steak strips in a single layer on a broiling pan. Broil on high for 5 minutes, or until the meat has reached the desired level of doneness.

Divide the cooked steak strips evenly among all 4 plates. Top with the caramelized onion and mushrooms.

PER SERVING: 765 Calories; 56g Fat; 47g Protein; 23g Carbohydrate; 8g Dietary Fiber; 15g Net Carbs

THREE-MEAT NO-BEAN CHILI

What? No beans? Chili has to have beans! That is the response I get every time I tell someone that my chili recipe does not contain beans. Let's be honest, if you had to choose between only meat or only beans, meat would win out every time! My chili gives you not one, but three different types of meat. Trust me when I tell you that you will not miss the beans. This recipe has won chili cookouts and stood up against a variety of versions that all contained beans. It is the real deal.

SERVES: 16

1½ lbs (680 g) ground beef

1 lb (455 g) ground turkey

1 lb (455 g) ground pork

5 large cloves garlic, minced

1 medium red onion, chopped

1 tbsp (20 g) sea salt

1½ tsp (4 g) black pepper

4 ribs celery, diced

⅓ cup (45 g) pickled jalapeño pepper, chopped

1 (6 oz [170 g]) can organic tomato paste

2 (15 oz [425 g]) cans diced organic tomatoes and green chiles, with juices

2 (15 oz [425 g]) cans diced organic tomatoes, drained

½ cup (75 g) orange bell pepper, chopped

½ cup (75 g) green bell pepper, chopped

¼ cup (60 ml) gluten-free Worcestershire sauce

4 tbsp (35 g) chili powder

3 tbsp (20 g) ground cumin

2 tsp (5 g) onion powder

2 tsp (7 g) garlic powder

2 tsp (4 g) dried oregano

1 tsp paprika

½ tsp cayenne pepper

Heat a slow cooker on the low setting.

In a large skillet over medium-high heat, combine the ground beef, ground turkey, ground pork, garlic, red onion, sea salt and pepper. Cook until all the meats are browned. Drain any excess grease and add the meat mixture to the slow cooker.

In the slow cooker, combine the celery, jalapeño, tomato paste, tomatoes and green chiles, diced tomatoes, orange and green bell pepper, Worcestershire sauce, chili powder, cumin, onion powder, garlic powder, oregano, paprika and cayenne pepper.

Mix until all the ingredients are well incorporated. Cover and cook for 6 to 8 hours.

PER SERVING: 598 Calories; 41g Fat; 38g Protein; 21g Carbohydrate; 5g Dietary Fiber; 16g Net Carbs

NOTE: I love to top this chili with some sharp cheddar cheese, sour cream and green onions. These optional garnishes are not included in the nutritional analysis.

BUFFALO CHICKEN WEDGE SALAD

The classic wedge salad used to be a staple on restaurant menus everywhere, and despite its popularity, it is rarely seen anymore. I'm bringing it back! For this version, I decided to fuse the classic wedge salad with the standard ingredients for Buffalo wings. This is a great way to make a salad into a full meal. I top this salad with the Creamy Chive Blue Cheese Dressing (page 174).

SERVES: 4

2 tbsp (30 g) butter

½ cup (120 ml) Buffalo wing sauce

12 oz (340 g) chicken breast, cooked and shredded

1 large head iceberg lettuce, quartered

½ cup (70 g) blue cheese crumbles

2 ribs celery, diced

½ cup (65 g) carrots, diced

1 medium tomato, diced

2 green onions, chopped

Creamy Chive Blue Cheese Dressing (page 174), for serving

In a medium saucepan over low heat, melt the butter. Once the butter is melted, mix in the Buffalo wing sauce. Toss the shredded chicken in the sauce until it is completely coated.

Top each iceberg wedge with the chicken, blue cheese crumbles, celery, carrots, tomato and green onions, and drizzle with the Creamy Chive Blue Cheese Dressing.

PER SERVING: 320 Calories (excluding the dressing); 23g Fat; 20g Protein; 9g Carbohydrate; 3g Dietary Fiber; 6g Net Carbs

ITALIAN CHOPPED SALAD

For years, I worked in an Italian restaurant. I was known to eat a chopped salad for lunch every day for weeks on end. It's a salad I never tire of. A good chopped salad transforms an antipasto tray into a meal. This salad does exactly that.

SERVES: 4

1 large head romaine lettuce, shredded

8 oz (230 g) chicken, cooked and cubed

5 oz (145 g) gluten-free salami, sliced into strips

6 slices bacon, cooked crisp and crumbled

1 cup (115 g) mozzarella cheese, shredded

⅓ cup (60 g) Kalamata olives, halved

⅓ cup (20 g) sun-dried tomatoes

⅓ cup (30 g) pepperoncini, sliced

⅓ cup (60 g) artichoke hearts, rough chopped

¼ cup (40 g) red onion, diced

2 green onions, chopped

In a large mixing bowl, combine the romaine lettuce, chicken, salami, bacon, mozzarella cheese, Kalamata olives, sun-dried tomatoes, pepperoncini, artichoke hearts, red onion and green onions.

PER SERVING: 422 Calories; 30g Fat; 26g Protein; 14g Carbohydrate; 5g Dietary Fiber; 9g Net Carbs

NOTE: The Balsamic Vinaigrette (page 194) complements this recipe perfectly.

BROCCOLI SLAW CHICKEN SALAD

The heartiness of the broccoli slaw makes this a good salad for make-ahead meal prep as it will retain its crunch and not get soggy throughout the week. The sweet tartness of the dried cranberries and the airy crunchiness of the walnuts really add a unique dynamic to this salad. Serve with the Creamy Avocado Citrus Dressing (page 185).

SERVES: 4

1 (12 oz [340 g]) package broccoli slaw (broccoli, carrots, red cabbage)

10 oz (285 g) chicken, cooked and cubed

¼ cup (30 g) dried cranberries

½ cup (50 g) walnuts

Sea salt and black pepper, to taste

Creamy Avocado Citrus Dressing (page 185)

In a large mixing bowl, combine the broccoli slaw, chicken, cranberries, walnuts, sea salt and black pepper. Toss with Creamy Avocado Citrus Dressing.

PER SERVING: 205 Calories; 15g Fat; 13g Protein; 5g Carbohydrate; 2g Dietary Fiber; 3g Net Carbs

PHILLY CHEESESTEAK SOUP

I took a classic comfort food sandwich and turned it into a soup that will leave you wondering why you ever needed the bread in the first place. If you still feel like you need the bread, try dipping the Cheddar Dill Biscuits (page 124) in your soup. Better yet, pour some soup over top of them, biscuits and gravy style.

SERVES: 8–10

1 lb (455 g) precooked roast beef, thinly sliced strips

4 cups (950 ml) beef stock

1 small green bell pepper, diced

1 small red bell pepper, diced

3 tbsp (15 g) fresh parsley, chopped

2 tbsp (30 ml) gluten-free Worcestershire sauce

1 tsp sea salt

1 tsp black pepper

3 tbsp (45 g) butter

1 medium onion, thinly sliced

6 oz (170 g) mushrooms, thinly sliced

3 cloves garlic, minced

4 oz (115 g) provolone cheese

½ cup (120 ml) heavy cream

Heat a slow cooker on the low setting.

In the slow cooker, combine the beef slices, beef stock, green and red bell pepper, parsley, Worcestershire sauce, sea salt and black pepper.

In a large sauté pan over low-medium heat, melt the butter. Add the onion, mushrooms and garlic. Sauté until the onion and mushrooms are nice and caramelized, about 20 minutes. Add to the slow cooker. Cover and cook for 6 hours.

To the slow cooker, add the provolone cheese and heavy cream. Mix until the cheese is melted and well mixed in. Cover and cook for 1 additional hour.

PER SERVING: 462 Calories; 28g Fat; 39g Protein; 11g Carbohydrate; 2g Dietary Fiber; 9g Net Carbs

BRUSSELS SPROUTS AND KALE CHOPPED SALAD

The delicate shreds of slightly bitter Brussels sprouts and kale paired with the sweet tartness of dried cranberries and finished with the citrusy Lemon-Garlic Vinaigrette (page 190) really make this fresh and vibrant salad come to life.

SERVES: 4

1 bunch lacinato kale, shredded

1 lb (455 g) Brussels sprouts, trimmed and shaved

3 large leaves red cabbage, shredded

½ cup (70 g) dry-roasted almond slices

⅓ cup (40 g) dried cranberries

⅓ cup (30 g) Parmesan cheese, grated

Lemon-Garlic Vinaigrette (page 190), for garnish

In a large mixing bowl, combine the kale, Brussels sprouts, cabbage, almonds, cranberries and Parmesan cheese. Toss with Lemon-Garlic Vinaigrette.

PER SERVING: 198 Calories (excluding the dressing); 12g Fat; 10g Protein; 18g Carbohydrate; 7g Dietary Fiber; 11g Net Carbs

CASHEW CHICKEN SALAD

The addition of bright, fresh red grapes really elevates this salad to the next level, and the crunchiness of the celery adds a nice contrasting texture. Two of my favorite ways to serve this are over fresh butter lettuce leaves and over sliced avocado.

SERVES: 4

1 lb (455 g) chicken, cooked and cubed

½ cup (55 g) cashews

1 rib celery, diced

12 seedless red grapes, halved

2 green onions, chopped

⅓ cup (75 g) mayonnaise, or more if desired

Sea salt and black pepper, to taste

Fresh butter lettuce leaves or sliced avocado, for serving

In a large mixing bowl, combine the chicken, cashews, celery, grapes, green onions, mayonnaise, sea salt and black pepper. Mix until all the ingredients are well combined and coated with the mayonnaise.

Serve over fresh butter lettuce leaves or sliced avocado.

PER SERVING: 404 Calories; 35g Fat; 17g Protein; 7g Carbohydrate; 1g Dietary Fiber; 6g Net Carbs

NOTE: Nutritional analysis does not include butter lettuce leaves or sliced avocado.

CHICKEN POT PIE SOUP

Chicken pot pie was another staple in our home while I was growing up. I would come running into the house after a long day of playing outside, and with one whiff, I would instantly know what was for dinner. I am taken back to another time as this soup cooks all day, filling the house with the familiar smells of childhood.

SERVES: 5

1½ lbs (680 g) chicken breast, cubed

4 cups (960 ml) chicken stock

2 ribs celery, chopped

2 medium carrots, chopped

3 cloves garlic, minced

1½ tsp (8 g) sea salt

1 tsp onion powder

1 tsp dried thyme

¾ tsp black pepper

1 cup (240 ml) heavy cream

¾ cup (100 g) frozen peas

½ cup (60 g) sharp cheddar cheese, shredded

Heat a slow cooker on the low setting.

In the slow cooker, combine the chicken, chicken stock, celery, carrots, garlic, sea salt, onion powder, thyme and black pepper. Cover and cook for 5 hours.

Add the heavy cream, peas and cheddar cheese and cook for 1 additional hour.

PER SERVING: 456 Calories; 32g Fat; 29g Protein; 10g Carbohydrate; 2g Dietary Fiber; 8g Net Carbs

THAI CUCUMBER NOODLE SALAD

This recipe gave me yet another excuse to pull out my spiral slicer. It is incredibly fresh and light, with bold, vibrant colors. I am a firm believer that you eat with your eyes first and this salad has all the right colors to reel you in and make your mouth water. This salad, paired with a protein, such as grilled prawns or chicken skewers, and the Thai Peanut Sauce (page 198) make this dish a complete meal.

SERVES: 4

2 medium cucumbers, spiral sliced

2 large red cabbage leaves, shredded

2 green onions, chopped

½ cup (75 g) red bell pepper, julienned

2 tbsp (20 g) toasted sesame seeds

½ cup (120 ml) Thai Peanut Sauce (page 198)

¼ cup (5 g) fresh cilantro, optional, for garnish

In a large mixing bowl, combine the cucumbers, cabbage, green onions, bell pepper and sesame seeds. Toss with the sauce before serving.

PER SERVING: 179 Calories; 12g Fat; 7g Protein; 11g Carbohydrate; 4g Dietary Fiber; 7g Net Carbs

HEARTY SLOW COOKER CLAM CHOWDER

This is my low-carb take on a classic New England clam chowder. In this recipe I used cauliflower florets to simulate the texture of the potatoes traditionally found in clam chowder. Using the cream cheese as well as the heavy cream gives this a nice, thick, silky texture.

SERVES: 10

3 (10 oz [285 g]) cans whole clams, with juice

1 cup (240 ml) clam juice

4 cloves garlic, minced

1 shallot, minced

1 small leek, cleaned, trimmed and sliced

3 ribs celery, diced

1 medium sweet onion, chopped

2 tbsp (60 g) butter

2 tsp (10 g) sea salt

1 tsp black pepper

1 tsp garlic powder

1 tsp dried thyme

2 bay leaves

8 oz (230 g) cream cheese, softened

1 cup (240 ml) heavy cream

3 cups (300 g) small cauliflower florets

8 slices bacon, cooked crisp and crumbled

Heat a slow cooker on the low setting.

In the slow cooker, combine the clams, clam juice, garlic, shallot, leek, celery, onion, butter, sea salt, black pepper, garlic powder, thyme and bay leaves. Let cook for 1 hour.

Add the cream cheese in small chunks. Stir in the heavy cream. Continue mixing until there are no visible clumps of cream cheese and all the ingredients are well incorporated. Let cook for 4 hours.

Add the cauliflower florets and crumbled bacon. Let cook for an additional 1 to 2 hours.

PER SERVING: 385 Calories; 26g Fat; 28g Protein; 11g Carbohydrate; 1g Dietary Fiber; 10g Net Carbs

LEMON CAPER TUNA SALAD STUFFED TOMATOES

When I prepare this, I make the tuna salad ahead of time to let the flavors of the onions, capers, lemon and mustard really come together. From time to time, I also like to make this with the Ranch Dressing from (page 193) in place of the mayonnaise. When coring the tomatoes, I save the pulp and use it on salads or in tomato sauce.

SERVES: 4

4 medium beefsteak tomatoes, about 2 lbs (910 g)

2 (7 oz [200 g]) cans of tuna, packed in water

2 tbsp (25 g) red onion, minced

2 tbsp (20 g) capers

½ medium lemon, juice and zest

½ cup (110 g) mayonnaise

2 tbsp (35 g) gluten-free spicy brown mustard

1½ tsp (5 g) garlic powder

Sea salt and black pepper, to taste

Cut a ½ inch (1.3 cm)-thick slice off the top of the tomatoes. Use a spoon to scrape out the seeds, pulp and juice, hollowing out the tomatoes.

In a mixing bowl, combine the tuna, red onion, capers, lemon juice, lemon zest, mayonnaise, mustard, garlic powder and sea salt and black pepper. Mix until all the ingredients are well incorporated.

Spoon the tuna mixture into the hollowed-out tomatoes, mounding slightly.

PER SERVING: 326 Calories; 27g Fat; 14g Protein; 12g Carbohydrate; 3g Dietary Fiber; 9g Net Carbs

NOTE: These tomatoes are also amazing served warm. Roast the cored tomatoes at 400°F (205°C) for 20 minutes, add the tuna mixture and bake for 10 additional minutes.

BACON SWEET POTATO TOTS

Tater tots bring another instant flashback to my childhood. Are you starting to see a theme here? Like a lot of my generation, I was raised on inexpensive cuts of meat, frozen vegetables and highly processed, packaged foods. As an adult, when I actually started to take a deeper look at ingredient lists of all these foods, I was appalled. Have you ever picked up a bag of frozen tots or even sweet potato fries? One would think the only necessary ingredients would be potatoes and maybe some seasoning. The ingredient list is long and hard to pronounce. I knew I had an opportunity to clean things up and make sure my family is eating nutrient-dense whole foods, without missing out on treats such as tots. In this recipe, which uses sweet potatoes, I bake them, but you can also fry them. I recommend making them ahead of time and freezing them first if you are going to fry them. I love to serve these with Creamy Horseradish Sauce (page 189).

SERVES: 5

2 large sweet potatoes

6 strips bacon, cooked crisp and crumbled

¼ cup (25 g) almond flour

1 tsp garlic powder

1 tsp sea salt

¾ tsp black pepper

Preheat the oven to 400°F (205°C). Line a rimmed baking sheet with parchment paper.

Bring a large pot of salted water to a boil. Boil the sweet potatoes for 15 minutes, cooking only partially. Remove from the water and let cool.

Using a box grater, grate the sweet potatoes into a large mixing bowl. Press paper towels into the grated sweet potatoes to soak up as much excess moisture as possible.

To the sweet potatoes add the crumbled bacon, almond flour, garlic powder, sea salt and black pepper. Mix until all the ingredients are well incorporated. Form the mixture into small logs.

Bake the tots for 40 minutes, or until they are nice and crispy on the outside.

PER SERVING: 101 Calories; 4g Fat; 3g Protein; 13g Carbohydrate; 2g Dietary Fiber; 11g Net Carbs

PROSCIUTTO-WRAPPED ASPARAGUS WITH HOLLANDAISE

I love vegetables. I also love meat. Anytime they make an appearance together, I am a happy girl. The light saltiness from the prosciutto combined with the buttery lemon flavor of the hollandaise sauce is a match made in heaven. I broil these on top of a cooling rack so that the prosciutto can crisp up all the way around. Another option would be to panfry these in a little olive oil to get them nice and crispy.

SERVES: 4

1 large bunch asparagus (about 25)

8 oz (230 g) prosciutto, thinly sliced

½ cup (120 ml) Hollandaise Sauce (page 178)

Preheat the oven on broil at 500°F (260°C). Line a rimmed baking sheet with a cooling rack.

Clean and trim the asparagus, if necessary. Wrap each spear tightly in a piece of prosciutto, starting from the bottom and working your way around to the top.

Line the wrapped spears in a single layer across the cooling rack. Broil for 10 minutes, or until the prosciutto is crispy.

Top with the hollandaise sauce before serving, or serve with the sauce on the side as a dip.

PER SERVING: 299 Calories; 22g Fat; 20g Protein; 7g Carbohydrate; 2g Dietary Fiber; 5g Net Carbs

SWEET AND SPICY GREEN BEANS

The subtle sweetness of the coconut sugar and the heat of the red pepper flakes really give these beans a great balanced flavor. This is one of those recipes that will make your side dish the star of the show.

SERVES: 4

1 lb (455 g) fresh green beans, cleaned and trimmed

¼ cup (60 g) butter (½ stick), melted and divided

2 tbsp (30 ml) olive oil

1 medium red bell pepper, thinly sliced

1 small onion, thinly sliced

2 cloves garlic, minced

Sea salt and black pepper

2 tbsp (30 ml) gluten-free soy sauce or coconut aminos

1 tbsp (10 g) coconut sugar

1 tsp crushed red pepper flakes

In a large pot of salted water, bring the green beans to a boil. Boil for 3 to 4 minutes. Drain in a colander and submerge the beans in an ice water bath to shock them and stop the cooking process. Drain and set aside.

In a large skillet over medium heat, heat 2 tablespoons (30 g) of the butter and the olive oil. Add the green beans to the pan, toss in the butter and olive oil, and sauté for 5 minutes. Add the bell pepper, onion, garlic, sea salt and black pepper to taste. Sauté for an additional 5 minutes.

In a small bowl, combine the remaining 2 tablespoons (30 g) of melted butter and the soy sauce, coconut sugar and red pepper flakes. Pour the mixture over top of the green beans and toss until they are well coated.

PER SERVING: 233 Calories; 19g Fat; 3g Protein; 14g Carbohydrate; 5g Dietary Fiber; 9g Net Carbs

STEAMED ARTICHOKES WITH LEMON-GARLIC AIOLI

Artichokes might be one of the most confusing foods in the world. I was never exposed to them as a child, and when I first encountered one, I was like, "I'm supposed to do what? That seems so wasteful." Little did I know, there was a deliciously meaty, nutty little gem waiting for me on the base of the leaves.

SERVES: 4

4 cups (960 ml) chicken stock

4 large artichokes

1 tbsp (10 g) dried onion flakes

1½ tsp (8 g) sea salt

1 cup (240 g) Lemon-Garlic Aioli (page 197)

Heat a large saucepot over medium-high heat and pour in the chicken stock.

Cut away ½ to 1 inch (1.3 to 2.5 cm) from the top of each artichoke. Remove any dead or brown outer leaves. Cut off the stems close to the base so that that artichokes will stand upright. Place the trimmed artichokes in the pot, sprinkle with the onion flakes and sea salt, cover and simmer for 30 minutes, or until the artichokes are tender and the leaves are easily plucked.

Serve with Lemon Garlic Aioli for dipping.

PER SERVING: 413 Calories; 38g Fat; 6g Protein; 18g Carbohydrate; 7g Dietary Fiber; 11g Net Carbs

CHEESY GARLIC CREAMED SPINACH

There is something so mouthwatering about pairing this spinach with a thick, juicy cut of steak. They complement each other perfectly. This spinach is also delicious stuffed inside of plump, tender chicken breasts and then baked.

SERVES: 4

3 tbsp (45 g) butter

4 cloves garlic, minced

2 lbs (910 g) fresh spinach leaves

Sea salt and black pepper, to taste

1 cup (240 ml) heavy cream

¼ cup (25 g) Parmesan cheese, grated

¼ cup (30 g) mozzarella cheese, shredded

¼ cup (30 g) goat cheese

In a large sauté pan over medium heat, melt the butter. Add the garlic and sauté for 1 minute, being careful not to burn it.

Add the spinach. Season with sea salt and black pepper. Sauté until the spinach is wilted. Remove the spinach from the pan and let it drain. You may need to press it in a colander to remove all of the excess moisture.

To the same pan, add the heavy cream, Parmesan, mozzarella and goat cheeses. Reduce the heat to low and allow the sauce to thicken, 5 to 10 minutes. Add the wilted spinach back to the pan and toss until evenly coated in the creamy cheese sauce.

PER SERVING: 416 Calories; 38g Fat; 13g Protein; 9g Carbohydrate; 4g Dietary Fiber; 5g Net Carbs

RAINBOW VEGETABLE NOODLES

These vegetable noodles are so incredibly versatile. I like to follow the recipe below and then leave them in the oven until they get nice and crispy and serve them as a hash with eggs. You can also sauté them in a pan with a little butter, olive oil, sea salt and black pepper for a nice al dente vegetable noodle. They are sure to add more vegetables and more color to your life.

SERVES: 6

4 tbsp (45 g) bacon fat, butter or cooking oil

1 medium zucchini

1 medium summer squash

1 large carrot

1 small sweet potato

1 small red onion

1 red bell pepper

3 large cloves garlic

Sea salt and black pepper, to taste

Tomato Cream Sauce (page 186), optional, for garnish

Preheat the oven to 400°F (205°C). Coat a rimmed baking sheet with the bacon fat.

Using a spiral slicer, slice the zucchini, summer squash, carrot and sweet potato into noodle-like ribbons.

Using a mandoline, on the thinnest setting, slice the red onion, bell pepper and garlic.

Combine all the vegetables, sprinkle with sea salt and black pepper and toss to mix.

Spread the vegetable noodles in a thin layer across baking sheet. Bake for 20 minutes, tossing after 10 minutes.

PER SERVING: 124 Calories; 8g Fat; 2g Protein; 13g Carbohydrate; 3g Dietary Fiber; 10g Net Carbs

PANCETTA PARMESAN RISOTTO

I just love a thick, creamy risotto. It is the kind of side dish that goes well with just about every type of protein. The bonus of making this with cauliflower rice is that it drastically reduces the cook time of a traditional risotto.

SERVES: 6

2 tbsp (30 g) butter

2 tbsp (30 ml) olive oil

10 oz (285 g) pancetta, diced

6 cloves garlic, minced

4 oz (115 g) onion, diced

2 cups (480 ml) chicken stock

4 cups (480 g) cauliflower, riced

¾ cup (180 ml) heavy cream

½ cup (50 g) Parmesan cheese, grated

3 tbsp (15 g) fresh parsley, chopped

In a large sauté pan, heat the butter and olive oil over medium heat. Add the pancetta. Cook until the pancetta is rendered down and nice and crispy. Using a slotted spoon, remove the pancetta from the pan and set aside.

To the pan, add the garlic and onion. Sauté until the onion is soft and the garlic is fragrant, about 5 minutes. Add the chicken stock and cauliflower. Sauté for 10 minutes, stirring often.

Add the heavy cream to the pan and bring to a boil over medium heat. Reduce the heat to low and allow the sauce to simmer and thicken. Once the sauce has thickened, stir in Parmesan cheese and parsley. Add the pancetta back to the pan and enjoy!

PER SERVING: 350 Calories; 27g Fat; 20g Protein; 8g Carbohydrate; 2g Dietary Fiber; 6g Net Carbs

BROWN BUTTER BALSAMIC BROCCOLI WITH MIZITHRA CHEESE

The browned butter adds a nice nutty flavor to this dish. Just be sure to keep an eye on it as it is cooking because it can go from brown to burnt in no time flat. Mizithra cheese has a mild but tart flavor that pairs nicely with the nutty flavor of the browned butter.

SERVES: 6

1 large head broccoli, cut into florets

2 tsp (10 g) sea salt, divided

6 tbsp (90 g) butter

3 tbsp (45 ml) balsamic vinegar

2 cloves garlic, minced

½ cup (60 g) mizithra cheese, shredded

Bring a large pot of water to a boil over high heat. Add the broccoli and 1 teaspoon of the salt to the pot. Boil until crisp-tender, 3 to 4 minutes. Plunge the broccoli in an ice water bath to stop the cooking. Drain and set aside.

In a large sauté pan over medium heat, melt the butter and heat it until it browns. Add the balsamic vinegar and garlic and reduce the heat to low.

Add the broccoli, sprinkle with the remaining teaspoon of sea salt and toss until heated and well coated in the sauce.

Top with the mizithra cheese before serving.

PER SERVING: 178 Calories; 16g Fat; 6g Protein; 6g Carbohydrate; 3g Dietary Fiber; 3g Net Carbs

ZESTY COLESLAW

Working in restaurants pretty much ruined coleslaw for me. If you have ever worked in a restaurant, then you know what I am talking about. It's the 5-gallon (20 L) buckets of slaw dressing that really did me in. It turned the cabbage into a dripping, soggy mess. I didn't eat it for years until I was making my Slow Cooker Pulled Pork (page 71), and I knew two things: It needed to be served with slaw and I could do this barbecue staple justice and make it from scratch. This recipe comes husband and kid approved.

SERVES: 10

½ cup (110 g) mayonnaise

½ cup (60 g) sour cream

2 tbsp (30 ml) apple cider vinegar

1 tbsp (15 g) gluten-free Dijon mustard

1 tsp celery salt

1 tsp onion powder

½ tsp black pepper

¼ tsp paprika

4 cups (1½ kg) green cabbage, shredded

2 cups (680 g) red cabbage, shredded

1 small red bell pepper, julienned

2 medium carrots, grated

In a large mixing bowl, combine the mayonnaise, sour cream, apple cider vinegar, mustard, celery salt, onion powder, black pepper and paprika.

Add the green cabbage, red cabbage, pepper and carrots. Toss until the slaw is well coated. Refrigerate for 1 hour prior to serving.

PER SERVING: 160 Calories; 11g Fat; 4g Protein; 15g Carbohydrate; 6g Dietary Fiber; 9g Net Carbs

SOUR CREAM AND ONION CAULIFLOWER MASH

Using an immersion blender or food processor to whip this cauliflower mash really helps give it a mashed potato–like feel. After mashing it by hand, I usually transfer it to my food processor and give it a few quick pulses until it is nice and smooth. Sour cream and onion have always been the go-to toppings for potatoes; they are equally as perfect a topping for cauliflower masquerading as potatoes. This mash is terrific served alongside the Old-Fashioned Meat Loaf (page 76).

SERVES: 8

1 large head cauliflower, cleaned and trimmed

3 cloves garlic, minced

¼ cup (60 g) butter (½ stick)

¾ cup (90 g) sour cream

¾ cup (75 g) Parmesan cheese, grated

¼ cup (15 g) chives, chopped

2 tbsp (30 g) gluten-free Dijon mustard

1 tbsp (10 g) dried onion flakes

Sea salt and black pepper, to taste

Fill a large covered saucepot with 1 inch (2.5 cm) of water and place it over high heat. Steam the cauliflower, whole and uncovered, until fork tender, about 15 minutes.

Once the cauliflower has finished cooking, drain the water from the pot. Leave the cauliflower in the hot pot, cover and put back on the stove. Let sit for 5 minutes to help draw out any excess moisture. This is an important step. If you skip this step, you could end up with cauliflower soup.

Fork mash the cauliflower in the pan. Add the garlic, butter, sour cream, Parmesan cheese, chives, mustard, onion flakes, sea salt and pepper. Mash until the cauliflower reaches a potato-like consistency and all the ingredients are well incorporated.

PER SERVING: 133 Calories; 11g Fat; 5g Protein; 3g Carbohydrate; 1g Dietary Fiber; 2g Net Carbs

LOADED CAULIFLOWER CASSEROLE

I don't know a single person who doesn't love a juicy, loaded baked potato. There is something magical that happens when cheese, sour cream, bacon and green onions come together. For this recipe I set out to re-create that magic and come up with a version just as comforting as the real thing.

SERVES: 6

1 medium head cauliflower, cleaned and trimmed

1 cup (240 ml) chicken stock

3 cloves garlic, minced

4 oz (115 g) cream cheese, softened

½ cup (60 g) sour cream

1 cup (115 g) sharp cheddar cheese, shredded

2 large green onions, chopped

8 strips of bacon, cooked crisp and crumbled

Sea salt and black pepper, to taste

Preheat the oven to 350°F (177°C).

In a large, covered pot over high heat, steam the head of cauliflower whole in the chicken stock until fork tender, about 15 minutes.

Drain the chicken stock and leave the cauliflower in the hot pot. Cover and let sit for 5 minutes. This will help draw out any excess moisture from the cauliflower.

In a large mixing bowl, fork mash the cauliflower and mix in the garlic, cream cheese and sour cream. Next, add the cheddar cheese, green onions, bacon, and sea salt and black pepper.

Transfer the mixture to a casserole dish and bake for 15 to 20 minutes.

PER SERVING: 226 Calories; 19g Fat; 10g Protein; 3g Carbohydrate; 1g Dietary Fiber; 2g Net Carbs

LEMON BLUEBERRY MUFFINS

I'm not sure that anything can make a home smell as heavenly as fresh baked blueberry muffins. That explains why there are so many blueberry muffin–scented candles out there. While most muffins are off limits for a primal low-carb lifestyle, thanks to alternative flours, we can take back muffins! For this recipe, there are a few substitutions you can make and still have these muffins turn out fantastic. You can substitute the butter with an equal amount of ghee or coconut oil. You can also swap the applesauce for one ripe, mashed banana.

SERVES: 10

1 cup (250 g) unsweetened applesauce

4 large eggs

¼ cup (60 g) butter (½ stick), melted

1 tbsp (6 g) lemon zest

1½ tsp (8 ml) vanilla extract

1 tsp lemon extract

½ cup (30 g) coconut flour

1 tbsp (10 g) coconut sugar

1 tsp ground cinnamon

½ tsp baking soda

½ tsp sea salt

½ cup (80 g) frozen blueberries

Preheat the oven to 350°F (177°C).

In a large mixing bowl, combine the applesauce, eggs, butter, lemon zest, vanilla and lemon extracts. Whisk together until all the ingredients are well incorporated.

In a separate bowl, combine the coconut flour, coconut sugar, cinnamon, baking soda and sea salt. Mix until the dry ingredients are well combined.

Add the dry ingredients to the wet ingredients and mix until all the ingredients are well incorporated and there are no visible clumps. Gently fold in the blueberries.

Lightly grease a 10-cup muffin tin or line with muffin cups. Divide the mixture evenly among the prepared cups. Bake for 25 to 30 minutes. Allow to cool on a cooling rack before serving.

PER SERVING: 108 Calories; 7g Fat; 3g Protein; 7g Carbohydrate; 2g Dietary Fiber; 5g Net Carbs

COFFEE-COCOA ROASTED NUTS

These nuts make for an excellent portable snack on the go. They are also a great way to curb that sweet tooth that plagues us all from time to time. During the holidays I like to make a triple batch and give them to family and friends.

SERVES: 14

1 cup (95 g) raw almonds

1 cup (130 g) raw cashews

1 cup (110 g) raw pecans

3 tbsp (45 g) butter, melted

2 tsp (9 g) vanilla extract

1½ tsp (7 g) coffee extract

3 tbsp (30 g) coconut sugar

3 tbsp (20 g) unsweetened cocoa powder

Preheat the oven to 350°F (177°C). Line a rimmed baking sheet with parchment paper.

In a large mixing bowl, combine the almonds, cashews and pecans.

In a separate bowl, combine the butter, vanilla and coffee extract. Mix in the coconut sugar and cocoa powder. Mix until all the ingredients are well combined and make a thick chocolate sauce.

Pour the mixture over the nuts and mix until the nuts are evenly coated with the sauce.

Line the nuts in a single layer across the parchment paper. Use a rubber spatula to scrape any additional sauce out of the bowl and drizzle it over the nuts.

Bake for 20 minutes. Let cool before serving.

PER SERVING: 181 Calories; 16g Fat; 4g Protein; 8g Carbohydrate; 2g Dietary Fiber; 6g Net Carbs

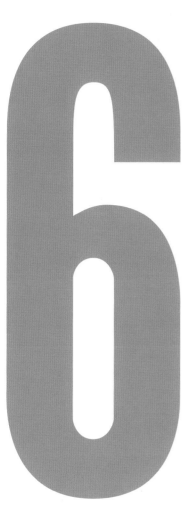

6 BREAKFAST

It is said that breakfast is the most important meal of the day. It gets you fueled up and ready to tackle what lies ahead. If you are anything like me, then you probably love traditional breakfast foods any time of the day. About once a week in our home, we have "Brinner"...Breakfast for dinner. Who says Biscuits with Country Sausage Gravy (page 157) can only be eaten during the day? I also love repurposing dinner leftovers and turning them into a spectacular breakfast dish. Who needs English muffins when you can have eggs benedict made on a base of dense, delicious crab cakes (page 162)? In this chapter you are sure to find some old classics, new favorites and everything in between.

SPICY SAUSAGE, SWEET POTATO AND TOMATO FRITTATA

The thing I love about frittatas is that they are an excellent way to use up leftovers. On Sunday mornings we usually use what is left from our food prep for the week and throw it into a big frittata. This has made for all different combinations of meat and vegetables. You know what? I have loved every single one. In fact, this recipe was created on a day when we were very low on groceries. It was beyond time to go shopping. I looked into the fridge and thought to myself, "What can I throw together with this last little bit of food in the house?" This was the result.

SERVES: 6

2 tbsp (30 ml) olive oil

1 lb (455 g) spicy pork sausage, ground

2 cups (270 g) sweet potato, diced

2 tsp (10 g) minced onion flakes

1 tsp garlic powder

1 tsp sea salt

½ tsp rubbed sage

12 large eggs

½ cup (60 g) mozzarella cheese, shredded

½ cup (50 g) Parmesan cheese, grated, divided

1 medium tomato, sliced in ½ inch (1.3 cm)-thick slices

2 tbsp (6 g) chives, chopped

Preheat the oven to 350°F (177°C).

In a large cast-iron skillet, heat the olive oil over medium-high heat. Add the sausage and sauté until browned.

Add the sweet potato, onion flakes, garlic powder, sea salt and sage. Mix to combine the ingredients and sauté for 5 to 10 minutes.

Crack the eggs into a large mixing bowl and fork whisk. Mix in the mozzarella cheese and ¼ cup (25 g) of the Parmesan cheese.

Pour the egg mixture into the skillet and stir with a rubber spatula. Let the eggs cook on the stove until the bottom has set and the top has started to set.

Top with sliced tomatoes, remaining Parmesan cheese and chives.

Transfer to the oven and bake for 15 to 20 minutes.

PER SERVING: 617 Calories; 50g Fat; 28g Protein; 12g Carbohydrate; 1g Dietary Fiber; 11g Net Carbs

BISCUITS AND COUNTRY SAUSAGE GRAVY

Nothing screams comfort quite like a nice, hot plate of biscuits and gravy. Both the biscuits and the gravy can be made ahead of time, making for a quick and easy morning. For the gravy recipe, I often use a maple flavored link sausage. The hint of sweetness is a great complement to the savory nature of this recipe. This gravy is also delicious on top of the Chicken-Fried Steak (page 47).

SERVES: 4

2 tbsp (30 g) butter

12 oz (340 g) pork breakfast sausage

⅔ cup (100 g) onion, diced

3 cloves garlic, minced

1½ cups (355 ml) heavy cream

1 tbsp (3 g) fresh parsley, chopped

½ tsp sea salt

8 Cheddar Dill Biscuits (page 124)

Heat the butter in a large skillet over medium heat. Once the butter is melted, add the sausage (crumbled if ground, sliced if using link sausage). Cook until the sausage is browned. Using a slotted spoon, remove the sausage from the pan, retaining the drippings. Set the sausage aside.

To the drippings in the pan, add the onion and garlic. Reduce the heat to medium-low and cook until the onion is translucent and soft. Stir often to avoid burning the garlic.

To the pan, add the heavy cream, parsley and sea salt. Increase the heat to medium and bring to a boil. Once the gravy begins to boil, reduce the heat to low and simmer. Once the gravy begins to thicken, add the sausage back to the pan.

Pour the sausage gravy over top of the biscuits and enjoy!

PER SERVING: 1,226 Calories; 118g Fat; 31g Protein; 16g Carbohydrate; 4g Dietary Fiber; 12g Net Carbs

BREAKFAST SAUSAGE

To do this sausage justice, it really needs to be made a day ahead of time. Doing this gives all the herbs a chance to really flavor the pork. I also like to make double or triple batches of these and freeze them. I have frozen them raw as well as cooked, but cooking them ahead of time and then freezing them makes for a quick weekday breakfast.

SERVES: 4

2 lbs (910 g) ground pork

2 tsp (2 g) rubbed sage

2 tsp (10 g) sea salt

1½ tsp (1 g) dried parsley

1 tsp garlic powder

1 tsp black pepper

½ tsp dried thyme

¼ tsp ground nutmeg

¼ tsp red pepper flakes

In a large mixing bowl, combine the ground pork, sage, sea salt, parsley, garlic powder, black pepper, thyme, nutmeg and red pepper flakes. Mix until all the ingredients are well incorporated. Cover and refrigerate for up to 24 hours. The more time you have to let it refrigerate, the more the flavors really come together.

Form mixture into patties and cook in a skillet over medium-high heat. Cook until both sides are golden brown, about 3 minutes each side.

PER SERVING: 151 Calories; 12g Fat; 10g Protein; trace Carbohydrate; trace Dietary Fiber; Trace Net Carbs

CHILI-CHEESE EGG MUFFINS

Consider these egg muffins a portable version of a chili-cheese omelet. I make these in an extra large muffin pan so that each muffin makes for a full serving. You can easily use a standard muffin pan and get a yield of 12 smaller muffins. This is another great make-ahead option for food prep days.

SERVES: 6

12 large eggs

2 cups (500 g) Three-Meat No-Bean Chili, (page 100)

1 cup (115 g) sharp cheddar cheese, shredded

⅔ cup (100 g) onion, diced

1 tsp sea salt

½ tsp black pepper

¼ cup (30 g) sour cream

¼ cup (15 g) chives, chopped

Preheat the oven to 350° (177°C). Lightly grease a muffin tin with 6 large (not standard-size) cups.

Crack the eggs into a large mixing bowl and fork whisk. To the eggs, mix in the chili, cheese, onion, sea salt and black pepper.

Divide the egg mixture evenly among the prepared cups. Bake for 20 to 25 minutes. Top with sour cream and chives before serving.

PER SERVING: 342 Calories; 24g Fat; 24g Protein; 6g Carbohydrate; 1g Dietary Fiber; 5g Net Carbs

NOTE: If you have extra chili laying around, why not pour some over the muffins before serving?

CRAB CAKE EGGS BENEDICT WITH CAJUN HOLLANDAISE SAUCE

Who needs English muffins when you can have deliciously, dense crab cakes jazzed up and covered in hollandaise sauce? This recipe is one of my favorite ways to repurpose crab cake leftovers and turn them into a spectacular breakfast dish.

SERVES: 4

1 cup (240 ml) Hollandaise Sauce (page 178)

1½ tsp (4 g) Blackened Seasoning (page 15)

8 large eggs

¼ tsp distilled white vinegar

8 Cajun Crab Cakes (page 38)

Mix the blackened seasoning into the hollandaise sauce and set aside.

Crack one of the eggs into a small bowl or ramekin.

Bring a small pot of water to a rapid boil. Add the vinegar to the water. Give the water a swirl to create a whirlpool effect. Gently, slip the egg into the center of the whirlpool. After 2 minutes, use a slotted spoon to remove the egg from the water.

Place the poached egg on top of a crab cake and cover with 2 tablespoons (30 ml) of the sauce. Repeat the process with each remaining egg and the remaining crab cakes and sauce.

PER SERVING: 827 Calories; 66g Fat; 51g Protein; 6g Carbohydrate; 1g Dietary Fiber; 5g Net Carbs

WAFFLE BREAKFAST SANDWICHES

The softer texture of these waffles makes for a perfect breakfast sandwich—the type of sandwich that is delicious for breakfast, lunch or dinner. I like to slather some mayonnaise on mine for a sweet and savory combo. This is also great with syrup drizzled over the top. Confession . . . I do both at the same time!

SERVES: 4

4 Cinnamon Waffles (page 169)

12 oz (340 g) Black Forest ham, thinly sliced and warmed

1 large avocado, peeled, pitted and sliced

4 slices sharp cheddar cheese

4 large eggs, fried

Mayonaise and/or maple syrup, for garnish

Cut each waffle in half, creating a top and bottom for the sandwich.

Layer 4 of the waffle halves with Black Forest ham, avocado, cheese and egg. Use the remaining 4 halves for the top of your sandwiches.

PER SERVING: 1,138 Calories; 90g Fat; 65g Protein; 26g Carbohydrate; 9g Dietary Fiber; 17g Net Carbs

LEMON CHIA PANCAKES

Chia seeds are high in fiber, rich in antioxidants and a great way to sneak in extra nutrients without increasing the overall carb count. These pancakes are light and fluffy with the fresh taste of lemon. Occasionally I like to add fresh blueberries and strawberries to the batter. Adding fresh fruit gives an extra burst of flavor.

SERVES: 3–4

½ cup (55 g) coconut flour

3 tbsp (30 g) coconut sugar

1 tsp ground cinnamon

½ tsp gluten-free baking powder

½ tsp sea salt

2 tbsp (15 g) lemon zest

2 tbsp (25 g) chia seeds

5 large eggs

¼ cup (60 g) butter (½ stick), melted

1 cup (240 ml) coconut milk

1 tsp vanilla extract

1 tsp lemon extract

1 tbsp (15 g) butter or oil, for cooking

In a large mixing bowl, combine the coconut flour, coconut sugar, cinnamon, baking powder, sea salt, lemon zest and chia seeds. Mix until the ingredients are well combined.

Crack the eggs into a separate bowl and whisk together with the melted butter, coconut milk, and vanilla and lemon extracts.

Slowly pour the egg mixture into the dry ingredients, a little at a time, mixing as you go. Mix until all the ingredients are well incorporated and there are no visible clumps.

Heat a large skillet over medium-high heat. Melt the butter in the pan. Once the butter is melted, pour ¼ cup (60 ml) of the batter at a time into the pan. Cook until the bottom is golden brown and the top begins to bubble, about 3 minutes. Carefully flip and cook until the other side is golden brown.

PER SERVING: 246 Calories; 20g Fat; 6g Protein; 12g Carbohydrate; 3g Dietary Fiber; 9g Net Carbs

CINNAMON WAFFLES

This recipe makes for a softer waffle than your traditional super-crisp Belgium variety. Personally, I prefer it that way as it saves the roof of my mouth from the torture that eating waffles usually inflicts. The subtle sweetness of these waffles makes them flavorful enough to eat plain. However, I like to top them with a little nut butter, syrup and sliced bananas.

SERVES: 4

½ cup (55 g) coconut flour

3 tbsp (30 g) coconut sugar

1 tsp ground cinnamon

½ tsp gluten-free baking powder

½ tsp sea salt

5 large eggs

¼ cup (60 g) butter (½ stick), melted

1 cup (240 ml) coconut milk

1 tsp vanilla extract

In a large mixing bowl, combine the coconut flour, coconut sugar, cinnamon, baking powder and sea salt. Mix until the ingredients are well combined.

Crack the eggs into a separate bowl and whisk together with the melted butter, coconut milk and vanilla extract.

Slowly pour the egg mixture into the dry ingredients, a little at a time, mixing as you go. Mix until all the ingredients are well incorporated and there are no visible clumps.

Ladle the batter into a greased, preheated waffle iron and cook until crisp and golden brown. This batter will take longer to get crispy than your normal waffle batter.

PER SERVING: 432 Calories; 35g Fat; 11g Protein; 20g Carbohydrate; 7g Dietary Fiber; 13g Net Carbs

KITCHEN SINK BREAKFAST SKILLET

I named this the Kitchen Sink Breakfast Skillet because as the old adage goes, it has everything in it but the kitchen sink. To lower the carb count even further, you can always omit the sweet potatoes from the recipe. Feel free to get creative with this recipe and use whatever meats and vegetables you have around your kitchen.

SERVES: 4

6 slices bacon, cooked crisp and crumbled

1 small sweet potato, diced

1 zucchini, halved lengthwise and sliced

10 black olives, sliced

3 mushrooms, thinly sliced

2 cloves garlic, thinly sliced

½ cup (75 g) red bell peppers, diced

½ cup (8 g) kale, chopped

½ cup (75 g) red onion, diced

2 tbsp (8 g) fresh parsley, chopped

1 tsp crushed red pepper flakes

Sea salt and black pepper, to taste

4 large eggs

¼ cup (40 g) feta cheese, crumbled

In a large cast-iron skillet over medium-high heat, cook the bacon until crispy. Remove the bacon from the pan and set aside, reserving the fat drippings in the pan.

To the fat drippings, add the sweet potatoes and sauté for 5 to 10 minutes. Add the zucchini, olives, bacon, mushrooms, garlic, bell peppers, kale, onion and parsley to the pan. Sprinkle the red pepper flakes, and sea salt and black pepper over the top. Sauté for 10 minutes more.

Crack the eggs on top of the sautéed vegetables. Cover and cook until the egg whites are cooked through and no longer runny.

Sprinkle feta cheese over the top before serving.

PER SERVING: 227 Calories; 13g Fat; 13g Protein; 15g Carbohydrate; 3g Dietary Fiber; 12g Net Carbs

7 DRESSINGS AND SAUCES

Dressings and sauces are some of my favorite recipes to make. There is something so rewarding about replacing the things that you normally buy store-bought versions of with your own scratch-made versions. Making popular condiments, dressings and sauces from scratch not only saves you money, they are so much healthier. They aren't packed with all the chemical additives and added sugars that are found in many of the store-bought varieties. When I make my dressings, I store in a mason jar with a pourable lid, and for the sauces, I typically make a double or even triple batch and freeze the extras.

How many bottles of expensive salad dressings do you think your family has gone through in the last year? Now, multiply that by the number of years you have been grocery shopping. That is a lot of dressing. Why not save money and get a better-tasting dressing by making such recipes as my Creamy Chive Blue Cheese Dressing (page 174) or Lemon Garlic Vinaigrette (page 190)?

CREAMY CHIVE BLUE CHEESE DRESSING

The pungent flavor of blue cheese and the mild onion flavor of the chives come together to create an extra layer of flavor not commonly found in your average blue cheese dressing. This recipe also works as a great dip. I like to serve it alongside a platter of fresh vegetables.

YIELD: 2 ½ CUPS (600 ML); SERVING SIZE: 2 TBSP (30 ML)

1 cup (220 g) mayonnaise

½ cup (60 g) sour cream

1 tbsp (15 ml) lemon juice

1 tsp Worcestershire sauce

1 tsp garlic powder

½ tsp sea salt

½ tsp black pepper

¾ cup (110 g) blue cheese crumbles

¼ cup (15 g) chives, chopped

In a medium mixing bowl, combine the mayonnaise, sour cream, lemon juice, Worcestershire sauce, garlic powder, sea salt and black pepper. Mix until all the ingredients are well incorporated.

Fold in the blue cheese crumbles and chives. Refrigerate, covered, for 1 to 2 hours before serving.

PER SERVING: 106 Calories; 12g Fat; 1g Protein; 1g Carbohydrate; trace Dietary Fiber; 1g Net Carbs

HEARTY MEAT SAUCE

This is another great recipe to sneak some leftover vegetables into. You can also use fresh herbs in place of the dried herbs. A good rule of thumb is that 1 teaspoon of dried herbs is equal to 1 tablespoon (4 g) of fresh herbs.

YIELD: 8 CUPS (1.9 L); SERVING SIZE: ½ CUP (120 ML)

1 lb (455 g) ground beef

8 oz (230 g) ground Italian pork sausage

½ cup (75 g) onion, diced

4 large cloves garlic, minced

1 tsp sea salt

2 (14 oz [415 mL]) cans organic diced tomatoes, with liquid

1 (14 oz [415 mL]) can organic tomato sauce

1 (6 oz [180 mL]) can organic tomato paste

8 oz (230 g) cremini mushrooms, thinly sliced

1 tbsp (3 g) fresh basil, chopped

1 tbsp (4 g) fresh parsley, chopped

1 tsp dried oregano

1 tsp dried Italian seasoning

1 tsp garlic salt

1 tsp onion powder

½ tsp crushed red pepper flakes

In a large skillet over medium-high heat, combine the ground beef, Italian pork sausage, onion, garlic and sea salt. Cook until the meat is browned. Drain any excess grease.

Transfer the meat mixture to a large saucepan. To the pan, add the diced tomatoes, tomato sauce, tomato paste, mushrooms, basil, parsley, oregano, Italian seasoning, garlic salt, onion powder and red pepper flakes. Mix until all the ingredients are well incorporated.

Reduce the heat to low and simmer, uncovered, for 30 minutes.

PER SERVING: 173 Calories; 14g Fat; 8g Protein; 6g Carbohydrate; 1g Dietary Fiber; 5g Net Carbs

HOLLANDAISE SAUCE

Hollandaise sauce is so simple but packs so much flavor. I love it on top of pretty much any breakfast. I have been known to just pour it over fried eggs. I even love it with dinner. It is great with a juicy steak or poured over broccoli. You just can't go wrong. When you are making this sauce, be careful not to let the eggs get too hot at any point or they will scramble and your sauce will not turn out well.

YIELD: 1 CUP (240 ML); SERVING SIZE: 2 TBSP (30 ML)

4 egg yolks

2 tbsp (30 ml) lemon juice

½ cup (120 g) butter (1 stick), melted

Dash of hot sauce

Pinch of cayenne pepper

Pinch of sea salt

In a stainless-steel mixing bowl, whisk the egg yolks and lemon juice together. The mixture should get thicker and increase in volume.

Heat a saucepan with 1 to 2 inches (2.5 to 5 cm) of water in it over medium heat until the water is simmering. Lower the heat to medium-low. Place the bowl over top of the saucepan, making sure that the water is not touching the bottom of the bowl or else the eggs will begin to scramble. Continue whisking rapidly.

Little by little, whisk in the melted butter until the sauce has thickened and is light and fluffy.

Remove from the heat and gently whisk in the hot sauce, cayenne pepper and sea salt.

PER SERVING: 132 Calories; 14g Fat; 2g Protein; trace Carbohydrate; trace Dietary Fiber; trace Net Carb

RUSSIAN DRESSING

Despite its name, Russian dressing was actually created in the United States. This sweet and tangy dressing pairs perfectly with a salty slab of corned beef. Drizzle it over the Reuben Stuffed Sweet Potatoes (page 75).

YIELD: 2 CUPS (480 ML); SERVING SIZE: 2 TBSP (30 ML)

1 cup (220 g) mayonnaise

½ cup (120 g) gluten-free ketchup (reduced sugar, organic preferred)

2 tbsp (30 g) gluten-free spicy brown mustard

1 tbsp (15 ml) gluten-free Worcestershire sauce

1 tbsp (4 g) fresh parsley, chopped

1 tbsp (3 g) fresh chives, chopped

1 tsp fresh dill, chopped

In a medium mixing bowl, combine the mayonnaise, ketchup, mustard, Worcestershire sauce, parsley, chives and dill. Mix until all the ingredients are well incorporated. Refrigerate for 1 to 2 hours before serving.

PER SERVING: 52 Calories; 6g Fat; trace Protein; trace Carbohydrate; trace Dietary Fiber; trace Net Carb

EASY PEASY PIZZA SAUCE

Making your own pizza sauce is incredibly easy and is a much healthier option. Have you ever read the ingredient label on a store-bought jar of sauce? There are a lot of ingredients on there that I don't even recognize and can hardly pronounce. Not only is this recipe simple to make, but there is a good chance you recognize these ingredients and already have all of them on hand.

YIELD: 1½ CUPS (360 ML); SERVING SIZE: 2 TBSP (20 ML)

1 (8 oz [240 mL]) can organic tomato sauce

1 (6 oz [180 mL]) can organic tomato paste

½ tsp dried oregano

½ tsp dried basil

½ tsp dried parsley

½ tsp minced onion flakes

½ tsp onion powder

¼ tsp garlic powder

¼ tsp sea salt

In a medium saucepan over low heat, add tomato sauce, tomato paste, oregano, basil, parsley, onion flakes, onion powder, garlic powder and sea salt. Simmer for 10 minutes.

PER SERVING: 18 Calories; trace Fat; 1g Protein; 4g Carbohydrate; 1g Dietary Fiber; 3g Net Carbs

SWEET AND TANGY BACON BARBECUE SAUCE

Before taking on the adventure of creating a low-carb barbecue sauce recipe, I took a poll among my readers. I simply asked, "When it comes to barbecue sauce, do you prefer it tangy or sweet?" It got over a thousand responses and the final tally was a pretty equal divide. People are serious about their sauce, especially in the South. I'll admit, I wasn't really sure which flavor profile I was setting out to create. I just started throwing things in the pot and tasting. It was a series of add, stir, taste, assess. In the end, I think I managed to capture both sweet and tangy. This sauce tastes tangy up front but finishes with a sweetness on the back. The addition of bacon is just icing on the barbecue.

YIELD: 3 CUPS (710 ML); SERVING SIZE: 2 TBSP (30 ML)

5 slices bacon

2 tbsp (30 g) butter

1 (15 oz [425 g]) can organic tomato sauce

1 (7 oz [200 g]) can organic tomato paste

½ cup (125 g) unsweetened applesauce

¼ cup (60 ml) apple cider vinegar

¼ cup (60 ml) coconut aminos

2 tbsp (30 ml) liquid smoke

1 tbsp (10 g) garlic powder

1 tbsp (10 g) minced onion flakes

1 tbsp (10 g) coconut sugar

2 tsp (6 g) chili powder

1 tsp gluten-free yellow mustard

½ tsp celery salt

¼ tsp sea salt

½ tsp black pepper

Pinch of ground cloves

Cook the bacon until it is nice and crispy, crumble and set aside. Retain 2 tablespoons (30 ml) of the drippings for the sauce.

Heat a saucepot over medium-low heat. In the pot, heat the bacon fat and butter.

Once the butter is melted, mix in the tomato sauce, tomato paste, applesauce, apple cider vinegar, coconut aminos, liquid smoke, garlic powder, onion flakes, coconut sugar, chili powder, mustard, celery salt, sea salt, black pepper and cloves.

Let simmer for 15 to 20 minutes, stirring often.

PER SERVING: 24 Calories; 1g Fat; 1g Protein; 3g Carbohydrate; trace Dietary Fiber; 3g Net Carbs

CREAMY AVOCADO CITRUS DRESSING

My love of avocados is vast and unending. The perfectly ripe avocado has a delicate, nutty flavor and smooth, buttery texture. Just writing this makes me want one. This dressing is on the thicker side. However, you can thin it out by adding a little water or cream.

YIELD: 3 CUPS (710 ML); SERVING SIZE: 2 TBSP (30 ML)

2 medium avocados, peeled, pitted and cubed

½ cup (110 g) mayonnaise

½ cup (60 g) sour cream

2 cloves garlic, minced

1 small lime, juiced

2 tbsp (30 ml) avocado oil

2 tbsp (3 g) dried parsley

1 tbsp (3 g) fresh chives, chopped

Sea salt and black pepper, to taste

In a food processor, combine the avocado, mayonnaise, sour cream, garlic, lime juice, avocado oil, parsley, chives, and sea salt and black pepper. Pulse until smooth and creamy.

PER SERVING: 77 Calories; 8g Fat; 1g Protein; 2g Carbohydrate; trace Dietary Fiber; 2g Net Carbs

TOMATO CREAM SAUCE

I keep things classic with basil, oregano and Parmesan, but I love adding a little cream. It gives the sauce a nice silky texture, without losing the robust taste of the tomatoes.

YIELD: 4½ CUPS (1 L); SERVING SIZE: ¼ CUP (60 ML)

1 (15 oz [425 g]) can organic stewed tomatoes

1 (15 oz [425 g]) can organic diced tomatoes

1 (6 oz [170 g]) can organic tomato paste

4 cloves garlic, thinly sliced

2 tbsp (6 g) fresh basil, chopped

1 tbsp (6 g) dried Italian seasoning

2 tsp (4 g) dried oregano

1 tsp sea salt

½ cup (120 ml) heavy cream

¼ cup (25 g) Parmesan cheese, grated

Heat a large saucepan over medium heat. In the pan, combine the stewed tomatoes, diced tomatoes, tomato paste, garlic, fresh basil, Italian seasoning, oregano and sea salt. Bring to a boil over medium heat and then reduce the heat to low.

Add the heavy cream and Parmesan cheese. Mix until all the ingredients are well incorporated. Simmer for 10 to 15 minutes, stirring frequently.

Remove from the heat and, using an immersion blender, blend the sauce until it is smooth. Alternatively, this can be done in an upright blender.

PER SERVING: 51 Calories; 3g Fat; 2g Protein; 5g Carbohydrate; 1g Dietary Fiber; 4g Net Carbs

NOTE: I like to double or sometimes even triple this recipe and freeze it in batches for later use. Then I reheat it on the stovetop. You can't even tell it was previously frozen.

CREAMY HORSERADISH SAUCE

Typically, when people think of horseradish sauce, their mind instantly gravitates toward steak. I love pairing this horseradish sauce with sweeter foods, such as Bacon Sweet Potato Tots (page 127). Sweet and spicy is where it's at! If you are using straight horseradish root in place of the creamy horseradish, I recommend cutting it down to 2 tablespoons (30 g) as it is much spicier.

YIELD: 1½ CUPS (355 ML); SERVING SIZE: 2 TBSP (30 ML)

1 cup (120 g) sour cream

¼ cup (60 g) creamy horseradish

2 tbsp (8 g) fresh parsley, chopped

1 tbsp (15 g) gluten-free Dijon mustard

½ tsp sea salt

In a mixing bowl, combine the sour cream, creamy horseradish, parsley, mustard and sea salt. Mix until all the ingredients are well incorporated.

PER SERVING: 25 Calories; 2g Fat; trace Protein; 1g Carbohydrate; trace Dietary Fiber; trace Net Carb

LEMON-GARLIC VINAIGRETTE

This is a fresh and light dressing that complements just about any salad. It is also an excellent marinade for chicken and fish. I prefer to use avocado oil for my vinaigrette recipes as it is a great healthy fat and has a much lighter taste.

YIELD: 2 CUPS (475 ML); SERVING SIZE: 2 TBSP (30 ML)

1½ cups (355 ml) avocado oil

Juice of 1 large lemon

6 cloves garlic, minced

2 tbsp (30 g) gluten-free Dijon mustard

1 tbsp (10 g) dried onion flakes

1 tsp sea salt

½ tsp black pepper

In a glass jar with a lid, combine the avocado oil, lemon juice, garlic, mustard, onion flakes, sea salt and black pepper. Tightly fasten the lid on the jar and shake well until all the ingredients are well combined. For best flavor, refrigerate for up to 24 hours before serving.

PER SERVING: 187 Calories; 21g Fat; trace Protein; 1g Carbohydrate; trace Dietary Fiber; 1g Net Carbs

RANCH DRESSING

You can never go wrong with a good ranch dressing. I put it on almost everything. I like to use this recipe as a base and get creative with it. Sometimes I add a little salsa. Other times I will add some crispy bacon. I've even added a couple of tablespoons of taco seasoning to it. The possibilities are endless.

YIELD: 2¼ CUPS (590 ML); SERVING SIZE: 2 TBSP (30 ML)

½ cup (110 g) mayonnaise

½ cup (60 g) sour cream

1 clove garlic, minced

1 tbsp (4 g) fresh parsley, chopped

1 tbsp (3 g) fresh chives, chopped

2 tsp (10 ml) apple cider vinegar

1 tsp fresh dill, chopped

½ tsp onion powder

¼ tsp sea salt

⅛ tsp black pepper

In a mixing bowl, combine the mayonnaise, sour cream, garlic, parsley, chives, apple cider vinegar, dill, onion powder, sea salt and black pepper. Mix until all the ingredients are well incorporated. Refrigerate, covered, for at least 1 hour before serving.

PER SERVING: 52 Calories; 6g Fat; trace Protein; trace Carbohydrate; trace Dietary Fiber; trace Net Carbs

BALSAMIC VINAIGRETTE

The great thing about a vinaigrette is that it takes no time to make and you can really get by without even measuring your ingredients. A little bit of this and a little bit of that goes a long way. Whenever I make vinaigrette, I always add Dijon mustard to help emulsify it.

YIELD: 2½ CUPS (590 ML); SERVING SIZE: 2 TBSP (30 ML)

1 cup (240 ml) balsamic vinegar

1 cup (240 ml) avocado oil

Juice of ½ lemon

1 small shallot, minced

1 clove garlic, minced

2 tbsp (30 g) gluten-free Dijon mustard

1 tsp crushed red pepper flakes

1 tsp onion powder

1 tsp sea salt

In a glass jar with a lid, combine the balsamic vinegar, avocado oil, lemon juice, shallot, garlic, mustard, red pepper flakes, onion powder and sea salt. Tightly fasten the lid on the jar and shake well until all the ingredients are well combined. Refrigerate for up to 24 hours before serving, for best flavor.

PER SERVING: 50 Calories; 5g Fat; trace Protein; 1g Carbohydrate; trace Dietary Fiber; 1g Net Carbs

LEMON-GARLIC AIOLI

Aioli is mayonnaise's zesty sibling. I use this in place of regular mayonnaise when a dish needs an extra kick. It is a terrific way to jazz up tuna salad, chicken salad and deviled eggs. It makes a great dip for fresh seafood, and my personal favorite use is as a dip for Steamed Artichokes (page 132).

YIELD: 1¼ CUPS (355 ML); SERVING SIZE: 2 TBSP (30 ML)

1 cup (220 g) mayonnaise

4 cloves garlic, minced

2 tsp (10 g) gluten-free Dijon mustard

2 tsp (10 ml) lemon juice

½ tsp onion powder

In a medium mixing bowl, combine the mayonnaise, garlic, mustard, lemon juice and onion powder. Mix until all the ingredients are well incorporated. Refrigerate, covered, for 1 to 2 hours before serving.

PER SERVING: 161 Calories; 19g Fat; trace Protein; 1g Carbohydrate; trace Dietary Fiber; 1g Net Carbs

THAI PEANUT SAUCE

This sauce is sweet with just a hint of spicy peeking through. I love to pair this with spicy dishes, such as blackened chicken or prawns. This sauce is the perfect dressing for the Cucumber Noodle Salad (page 116).

YIELD: 2 CUPS (475 ML); SERVING SIZE: 2 TBSP (30 ML)

1 cup (260 g) chunky natural peanut butter

¼ cup (60 ml) coconut milk

¼ cup (60 ml) water

Juice of ½ lime

2 cloves garlic, minced

¼ cup (60 ml) gluten-free soy sauce or coconut aminos

1½ tsp (8 ml) rice vinegar

1 tsp sesame oil

1 tsp ginger, grated

½ tsp crushed red pepper flakes

In a medium mixing bowl, combine the peanut butter, coconut milk, water, lime juice, garlic, soy sauce, rice vinegar, sesame oil, ginger and crushed red pepper flakes. Whisk together until all the ingredients are well combined and smooth.

PER SERVING: 122 Calories; 9g Fat; 5g Protein; 4g Carbohydrate; 1g Dietary Fiber; 3g Net Carbs

ARTICHOKE TARTAR SAUCE WITH CAPERS

The tart, briny nature of the artichokes and capers makes them a natural choice for a guest appearance in a tartar sauce recipe.

YIELD: 2½ CUPS (590 ML); SERVING SIZE: 2 TBSP (30 ML)

1 small pickle, chopped

2 cloves garlic, minced

1½ cups (330 g) mayonnaise

¼ cup (40 g) onion, diced

2 tbsp (30 g) gluten-free spicy brown mustard

1 tbsp (15 ml) + 1 tsp lemon juice

1 tbsp (4 g) fresh parsley, chopped

1 tsp fresh dill, chopped

½ tsp sea salt

¼ tsp black pepper

⅓ cup (60 g) artichoke hearts, chopped

3 tbsp (30 g) capers

In a food processor, combine the pickle, garlic, mayonnaise, onion, mustard, lemon juice, parsley, dill, sea salt and black pepper. Give a few quick pulses until the ingredients are well combined but the chunks of pickle are still visible.

Add the artichokes and give a few more quick pulses. Using a rubber spatula, fold in the capers. Refrigerate, covered, before serving.

PER SERVING: 123 Calories; 14g Fat; trace Protein; 1g Carbohydrate; trace Dietary Fiber; 1g Net Carbs

ACKNOWLEDGMENTS

TO MY HUSBAND, JON

Thank you for your constant love and support through the turmoil of completing this project and for always being understanding when I had to skip family functions, social engagements and pretty much everything else in an attempt to focus on my work. With you in my corner, I know that anything is possible. Thank you for being my best friend, my biggest supporter and the love of my life.

TO MY SISTER, PAMELA

Thank you for consistently reminding me of my value and worth and always being my port in the storm. I love you to the moon and back.

TO MY DEAR FRIEND ERIN

Thank you for always having an open ear and an open heart. Your friendship and support though all that life throws our way has been immeasurable and I feel blessed to have you in my life.

TO MY FELLOW PAGE STREET AUTHORS

Thank you Stephanie, Ciarra and Rachael for letting me ask you all a million questions during this process. Without your patience and humor, I would have likely been bald by the time I finished this project.

TO THE PAGE STREET EMPLOYEES

Thank you for taking a chance on me, believing in my work and giving me this incredible opportunity. I am excited to see what the future holds. I have no doubt that I made the right decision in signing as a Page Street author.

ABOUT THE AUTHOR

Kyndra Holley is the founder of the wildly popular blog *Peace, Love and Low Carb* and the author of several self-published cookbooks. She is born and raised and still resides just outside of Seattle, Washington.

She is a self-taught home cook, passionate about living a primal low-carb lifestyle and helping others to do the same. Through this way of eating and her love of lifting heavy things, she has managed to lose nearly 60 pounds (27 kg). Her aim is to consistently create delicious, whole food recipes that leave you feeling satisfied.

When she is not in the kitchen, she can often be found in the gym, out on a long walk, playing with her four pups, teaching others about essential oils or traveling to destinations far and wide.

INDEX